D0176478

KNOWING THE
ECONOMY
OF GOD

How to Apply God's Financial Principles to Your Normal and Everyday Life

Truly I say to you, this poor widow put in more, than all the
contributors to the treasury; for they all put in out of their surplus,
but she, out of her poverty, put in all she owned, all she had to live on.
Mark 12:43,44 NASB

THOMAS MEAGLIA

PRESS
ACW Press
Nashville, TN 37222

Scripture quotations are taken from the following Bible Translations:

The New American Standard Bible ®, © 1960, 1962, 1963, 1968, 1971, 1972, 1973, 1975, 1977, 1995 by The Lockman Foundation. Used by permission. (www.Lockman.org)

The HOLY BIBLE, NEW INTERNATIONAL VERSION®. NIV®. Copyright©1973, 1978, 1984 by the International Bible Society. Used by permission of Zondervan. All rights reserved.

The King James Version of the Bible.

Knowing the Economy of God
Copyright ©2006 Thomas Meaglia
All rights reserved

Cover Design by Alpha Advertising
Interior Design by Pine Hill Graphics
Front Cover Artwork by Fred Smith – www.fredsmithart.com

Packaged by ACW Press
P.O. Box 110390
Nashville, TN 37222
www.acwpress.com
The views expressed or implied in this work do not necessarily reflect those of ACW Press. Ultimate design, content, and editorial accuracy of this work is the responsibility of the author(s).

Publisher's Cataloging-in-Publication Data
(Provided by Cassidy Cataloguing Services, Inc.)

Meaglia, Thomas.

   Knowing the economy of God : how to apply God's financial
   principles to your normal and everyday life / Thomas Meaglia. -- 1st
   ed. -- Nashville, TN : ACW Press, 2006.

     p. ; cm.

     ISBN-13: 978-1-932124-74-3
     ISBN-10: 1-932124-74-8

     1. Finance, Personal--Religious aspects. 2. Financial security--
   Religious aspects. 3. Stewardship, Christian. 4. Spirituality.
   5. Christian life. I. Title.

HG179 .M43 2006
332.024--dc22   0605

All rights reserved. No part of this book may be reproduced, stored in a retrieval system, or transmitted in any form or by any means—electronic, mechanical, photocopying, recording, or otherwise—without prior permission in writing from the copyright holder except as provided by USA copyright law.

Printed in the United States of America.

*To my Lord and Savior, Jesus Christ,
to whom I give glory, honor, and full
credit for the writing of this book.*

*Thank you, Almighty God,
for giving me the opportunity to help
others apply your financial truths and
principles to their everyday lives.*

CONTENTS

Examples of Stewardship
Seeking Counsel
Investing
Risk Management
Faithfulness
Taxes
Cheating and Stealing
Bankruptcy
One Body, Many Members
The Final Accounting

INTRODUCTION

Knowing *the Economy of God* is a book that teaches us how to manage our financial affairs in light of God's Word. God's economy is known as the methods, principles, rules, and standards He uses to teach us about His character. Following these rules will draw us closer to Him by obedience and will teach us to submit to the lordship of Christ in the financial areas of our lives.

God's economy works differently than the human systems men create in order to run societies the way they wish to operate them. Over the centuries, mankind has created standards in order to serve his own conceived purposes for a variety of reasons. These standards are not necessarily unbiblical or wrong; however, they clearly usurp the authority God should have in our lives. This book places God as the authority of all things. The only way to understand the economy of God is to study the Scripture He has given us which is 100 percent true and has the answers for today's living. Believing God's Word to be infallible plays a valuable part in bringing Him glory.

Some readers might be thinking, "How do you think you know what the mind of God is?" I do not know the mind of God, but I do know what He has written in the Bible. We interpret what it says, acknowledging both the context and the meaning. Then we consider how to apply the lesson to our daily everyday activities such as going to school, working, relaxing, or managing our budgets. We are God's tools, and it is His right to use us when and where He wants to. As believers, we need to be flexible, willing to be molded into what He sees fit for us. This book is designed to help us understand the principles of God's economy and how to apply those principles to the various areas of our life.

The great thing about God is that He helps us apply these concepts whether we are young or old, men or women, married or single. Our status does not matter. What a merciful, gracious God we serve! We know that we love God because He first loved us. Our response should be utter gratitude.

After watching the Passion of the Christ our hearts cried out, "Thank You, Jesus. We are so grateful to You!" That movie evoked a sense of indebtedness we feel for our Savior, so should we not want to obey what God teaches about how His economy works? Of course we do. We just need to understand what it says and its principles. Once we have the training, obedience becomes the key issue. We have to put into practice what He has taught us. Obedience does not come from our net worth or lack of it, but a *desire* to obey. When our kids break a rule, we do not cut off our relationship with them. It is the same in the family of God. We may fail, but the Lord gives us another chance. He does not give up on us. Let us appreciate His grace!

This book discusses how financial issues are related to scriptural lessons. We may not always follow these lessons, but we need to examine the Bible, believe what it says, and learn how to apply its teachings to our lives. From Genesis to Revelation, let's discover the wonderful blessings the Lord has in store for us.

If we were able to obey God's rules without any help from Him, we would not need His grace. Because we all fall short in our walk with God, we count on His grace and forgiveness. A second opportunity to obey and trust Him is granted to every evangelical born-again believer.

We want to do right in our Christian walk, and apply different lessons learned from Scripture to our normal, everyday life. But emotional or psychological problems hinder our application. There have been times we wanted to obey what the Bible said, but couldn't. For example, we had an opportunity to give time or money to someone, but never got around to it. Knowing and doing are two different things. There's an old phrase, "If I had a nickel for every time I did such and such, I would be rich." We do not always do what we know we should. This is why we must rely on the Spirit of God, and ask Him for strength, courage, and guidance to accomplish what He has asked. Trusting the Lord means we don't need to know the outcome of a situation or be in control of an event. Not being in control means we have released the reins to God.

So let's begin our journey. This adventure consists of obedience to God in the way we live for Him while having an attitude of thankfulness. The Lord's blessings are assured by obeying Him. However, blessings do not always come in monetary value, as many of us are prone to think. God does bless us with material things, but whether He does or not is left up to His discretion. A vital question to ask yourself is: "Do I obey God because of what I can get from Him, or do I obey and love Him because He gave me Jesus?" We need to understand that *not* receiving financial rewards might be exactly what is necessary for our walk with Christ to flourish. God wants us to grow in Him! Spiritual growth in light of His image is important, because relying on Him moves His heart. And let us not forget the blessings we *cannot* see! There are many treasures being laid up for us in heaven when we obey Christ's commands— treasures much richer than we can fathom!

God has given us an opportunity to be a part of His plan, to think like Him, and to be His disciple. Our status in life is not dependent on *if* He will choose us. We are *all* a part of His plan, His economy. What thrill it will be to meet someone in heaven who received his salvation partly due to our efforts to evangelize and support ministries that bring people to Christ? Now that is real joy! What could be more exhilarating? This should be our response to God because of His incredible and never-ending love for us.

If you have any thoughts as you read through this book, please do not hesitate to call. I welcome your comments. I do not claim to know it all, and I am certainly open for reproof.

A Note to the Reader

Please reflect on the following prayer before beginning this book.

Prayer of Foundation

Almighty God, Creator of the universe, and my loving heavenly Father, thank you first and foremost for giving me Jesus Christ, who saved me by grace. Not by my works, Lord God, but by your grace through faith I have been saved.

Thank you, Jesus, for your Word, your complete truth. I want to follow your instruction. Help me to continue to obey and follow the teachings and economic concepts found in your Word. And help me abolish the things I do that are sinful or unbiblical in any way.

Father God, help me to change what I do if it is not parallel with the Bible, especially concerning any financial issue or economic principle that would not bring glory to you. Help me glorify your name through money-related gifts and blessings you have given me so that people will come to Christ.

Also, I pray for help in following the example of Jesus, who I know as my Savior and Lord. I put away man's systems and economic ideas if they challenge or disagree with your Word. And, Almighty God, I know my security is built within you, not within any asset, accumulated thing, or job title. In Jesus' name—the Name above all names. Amen

Now that we know what the economy of God is, let us ask ourselves if we are already doing things that are right according to God? Or do we need to change in certain areas? What if He shows us things we are doing that are not right according to biblical authority, and we do *not* want to change?

Let our prayer be that the Holy Spirit will convict us and we will change accordingly. Let's have a go at this! Read on, brothers and sisters. Jesus is our example to follow and the Bible is our compass.

Remember that when we do not follow God's commandments, we sin. Fellowship is broken, and repentance is necessary. We must show an attitude of remorse if we want to restore communion with God the Father.

If Jesus Christ is Lord and Savior of our lives, we must die to our sinful nature just as Christ died for our sins. We are to make Him Lord of all parts of our lives, not just the parts we choose to surrender to Him. We cannot take the Bible and apply the parts we like and discard the others. We must make an effort to submit *every* aspect of our life to God if we want to be sanctified. Because we become more Christ-centered and less human involved, submitting helps us to build better relationships. We begin to look out for other's interests, not just our own. And because financial concepts are so often discussed in the Bible, we see just how important God's economy is. If we were not in a spiritual college, trying to learn what the Teacher is teaching, why else would this topic be so prevalent throughout Scripture?

We have two choices: to let the Holy Spirit lead us, or willfully disobey. We do not want to be caught up in legalism or use God's grace as a license to sin, so we learn what God's will is, apply it to our lives, and reap the blessings. Before we know it, we are loving love God with all our heart, soul, mind, and strength. The people around us will be able to see that our heart has been transformed. They will witness the fruit of the Spirit overflowing in our life. The Lord places far more value on qualities such as love, joy, peace, and patience than on money or material objects. We can develop these qualities by listening to His Word and doing what it says. Reading the Bible helps us to know God better and understand His mind more deeply. Let's start our personal study through the Bible, searching for economic and financial lessons to learn what the economy of God is. Let's also be willing to change if our lives reflect discrepancies according to these lessons.

The Four Anchors

We are first going to look at four anchors—the four major sections of God's economy: ownership, giving, stewardship, and contentment. These four areas are the key to understanding how the economy of God works as through them we learn how to give back to the Almighty Creator. Our purpose in life is to praise the Lord with our thoughts, actions, and words.

This book places the emphasis first on the Lord, the Supreme Authority above all, and then focuses on the ways we can glorify Him through the way we live. Our job is to be a good steward of the materials and abilities the Lord has given us to manage. We can give back to God on a day-to-day basis by learning to be a faithful manager. Having a positive attitude about where the Lord has specifically placed us in our life gives us another opportunity to obey and please Him with every waking breath.

It is my hope that you will find this book valuable to your everyday walk because of its rich scriptural content and the practical applications it offers. Above all, I desire that you leave your heart open and vulnerable to the work the Lord may accomplish in you through this book. If your heart is tender and ripe, you will definitely glean important and practical lessons. Be genuine; let the Holy Spirit correct and train you. We are all in this journey together, so let's get started!

The Recipe

Here is the recipe for studying *The Economy of God*:

1) Cite and read the scripture from the Bible.
2) Make sure there is an economic or money-related lesson. In other words, what is the economic principle from God?
3) Application. How does this lesson apply to everyday life? How should I change the way I live to glorify God and make Jesus Lord of the financial part of my life?
4) Pray the "prayer of change." Once we know what God's economy is, we need to allow His Spirit to guide us and help us abide in His ways.

Part 1
OWNERSHIP

GOD—THE SUPREME OWNER

Economic Principle:
everything belongs to the Lord.

*The earth is the LORD's and everything in it, the world,
and all who live in it; for he founded it upon the seas
and established it upon the waters.* Psalm 24:1-2

*The man without the Spirit does not accept the things
that come from the Spirit of God, for they are foolishness to him, and he cannot understand them, because
they are spiritually discerned. The spiritual man makes
judgments about all things, but he himself is not subject
to any man's judgment. "For who has known the mind
of the Lord that he may instruct him?" But we have the
mind of Christ.* 1 Corinthians 2:14-16

*"The silver is mine and the gold is mine," says the LORD
Almighty.* Haggai 2:8

*Remember the LORD your God, for it is he who gives
you the ability to produce wealth.* Deuteronomy 8:18

*Rich and poor have this in common: The LORD is the
maker of them all.* Proverbs 22:2

*"Beware that you do not forget the LORD your God by
not keeping His commandments and His ordinances
and His statutes which I am commanding you today;
otherwise, when you have eaten and are satisfied, and*

*have built good houses and lived in them, and when
your herds and your flocks multiply, and your silver and
gold multiply, and all that you have is multiplied, then
your heart will become proud and you will forget the
LORD your God."* Deuteronomy 8:11-14

*"So then, none of you can be My disciple who does not
give up all his own possessions."* Luke 14:33

*For every animal of the forest is mine, and the cattle on
a thousand hills. I know every bird in the mountains,
and the creatures in the field are mine. If I were hungry
I would not tell you, the world is mine, and all that is in
it.* Psalm 50:10-12

*Yours, O LORD, is the greatness and the power and the
glory and the majesty and the splendor. For everything
in heaven and earth is yours. Yours, O LORD, is the
kingdom; you are exalted as head over all. Wealth and
honor come from you; you are the ruler of all things. In
your hands are strength and power to exalt and give
strength to all.* 1 Chronicles 29:11-12

The earth is the Lord's, and everything in it.
1 Corinthians 10:26

*To the LORD your God belong the heavens, even the
highest heavens, the earth and everything in it.*
Deuteronomy 10:14

*If I have put my trust in gold or said to pure gold, "You
are my security," if I have rejoiced over my great wealth,*

the fortune my hands had gained…then these would also be sins to be judged, for I would have been unfaithful to God on high. Job 31:24-25,28

The economic principle taught in the above verses is that the Lord is the true owner of us and any property under our control. So, too, our time, talents, and bodies belong to God. They cannot be half ours and half God's, or a constant shift of power between ownership. It is all His. He made it, provided it, controls it, and owns it.

Webster's dictionary says that ownership means "to possess, belong to oneself; to hold or have as property." And secular viewpoints teach us that whoever controls something owns it. But in God's economy this is not the case. We may think we are controlling something when, in fact, the Lord is. He holds the deed to 100 percent of everything ever created, including you and me. The Bible clearly and accurately states this thesis, as we have seen in the cited verses. Now, how do we honor and glorify God, choosing to demonstrate Him as owner of our lives?

First, we must be willing to change how we live. After you pray the "prayer of change," you should take the necessary steps to live God's way, whether that means giving up a bad habit, learning to speak kindly to your wife or husband, or completely renovating your entire lifestyle.

This process is similar to quitclaiming a house deed. Quitclaiming means a person hands over ownership of a house to someone else, acknowledging he no longer has authority over decisions regarding it or even the freedom to enter at his whim. The new owner becomes the landlord and decides exactly what he wants to do to fix it up. This is essentially what we do when we make Jesus our Savior. Because He is Lord, we must do what He says to do: Luke 14:33 "So then, none of you can be My disciple who does not give up all his own posses-sions." Do you want to be Jesus' disciple? Let Him be the owner.

We are to live a life of one who does not have his security wrapped up in material things. God has clearly said we are not to have any idols before Him. If we allow anything or anyone to take the number one position other than Jesus, we are wor-shiping an idol.

Second, we must remember that life is made up of deci-sions—big and small. We will make more right decisions if we read the Bible every day and discover God's character. Every day we will be learning what better pleases Him and how to go about doing it. Anyone can say he agrees with the things of God, but how that person lives and the changes that take place in his life show us if he is abiding with Christ.

An owner of a business knows the intricate details of his store. He keeps painstakingly detailed records of all his spend-ing and earning transactions. God does the same thing in His economy. He keeps track of us, He knows our sitting down and our going out. He is familiar with all of our ways (Psalm 139:1-3). So, if the Lord is careful with His assets, shouldn't we be the same with ours? We should keep records of the money we make and the money we spend. Being well-acquainted with the numbers in the checkbook never hurts; it only keeps us well-informed and, hopefully, less likely to give in to careless spending. Take the qualities a good owner has and apply them in your life. Surrender them all to Christ, and He will help you learn to master those attributes according to His will.

Prayer of Change

Almighty God, you are a wonderful and very per-sonal God. You are the one true owner of everything I possess. Right now, I would like to take the time to acknowledge that everything I have belongs to you. You are in control, Jesus; I am just a vessel to carry out your purposes. Help me to use what you have given me to further your kingdom and my relationship with you. Even in the hard times, when money is scarce and I may doubt your presence, I believe that you will always provide for me according to how you want your name to be glorified. You may add and take away as you see fit, Lord, because I trust in your providence. I submit to you completely and return ownership of my life to you. I pray this in Jesus' name. Amen.

CREATION

Economic Principle:
God stamps His seal of ownership on everything created.

In the beginning God created the heavens and the earth.
Now the earth was formless and empty, darkness was
over the surface of the deep, and the Spirit of God was
hovering over the waters. Genesis 1:1-2

Several things are revealed in these two verses. In order to be faithful to God with something, there has to be something to be faithful with! If God did not create anything to honor Him, who or what would? So God created. He is the patent holder of the world because He is the inventor. We also understand that these verses say that everything is about God and not us. Life is not about us because *God* created. *He* is the supreme being of the universe. Logic tells us that He must have had a plan in mind when He made everything.

For the science gurus reading this book, check out the Web site, Reasons to Believe, at www.reasons.org. Here you will find materials and insight to convince any skeptic of the validity of creation. This Web site has the evidence to prove that creation by God truly happened.

The lesson to learn here is that we should worship God and not His creation. Beautiful oceans are enjoyable to look at, but they should not be worshiped in and of themselves. Let's praise and thank God the Creator for His work. His creation is a blessing, not an idol. We praise *God* for what He made.

In light of this principle, how should we change our lives? By realizing that God has a plan for our lives that includes worshiping Him, we can remove our focus from "things" and put it back on God.

God is powerful and artistic. If we build, design, draw, or illustrate, we must remember that He made us and gave us those talents of creativity. Thank the Lord if you have an artistic gift.

One of the ways of getting to know the different sides of God is to see Him as Creator. If we have not already, we need to alter any ungrateful attitude we have that separates us from enjoying God's blessings. It is easy to forget that He created the beautiful landscapes we witness every day. We get wrapped up in our own issues and become oblivious to the evidence of God as Creator. This causes us to doubt His presence! Let's not insult God by doubting His existence or His capability of making mountains; instead, let's receive the blessing of peace and joy in knowing the Creator intimately.

Prayer of Change

Almighty God, thank you for creating everything. I love and praise you for that. If you had not created me, I would have no existence! I credit you alone. I praise you, not the work of your hands. I do not need to understand how you made everything; I trust that you did because the Bible says so. Understanding that I am part of your overall plan, I pray in Jesus' name. Amen.

Economic Principle:
we are created to reflect the Master's character.

So God created man in his own image, in the image of God he created him; male and female he created them.

God blessed them and said to them, "Be fruitful and increase in number; fill the earth and subdue it. Rule over the fish of the sea and the birds of the air and over every living creature that moves on the ground." Then God said, "I give you every seed-bearing plant on the face of the whole earth and every tree that has fruit with seed in it. They will be yours for food. And to all the beasts of the earth and all the birds of the air and all the creatures that move on the ground—everything that has the breath of life in it—I give every green plant for food." And it was so. God saw all that he had made, and it was very good. And there was evening, and there was morning—the sixth day. Genesis 1:27-31

These verses speak volumes! The principle we learn here is that God created us in His likeness. We also find the first blessing, along with the first commandment in history: "Be fruitful and increase in number." Does a baker make a loaf of bread to set it on a shelf and stare at it? No, he creates it for a purpose: to be eaten. Does a builder build a house only to leave it empty? No, it is meant to provide shelter for a family. We were also created with a purpose: We are to fill the earth and rule over it.

In verse 31, God says that everything He made is good and He specifically created those things for us to enjoy. He provides our sustenance and gives a purpose for living. God is the giver; we are just the blessed recipients. We receive the command to inhabit the earth. We have a responsibility to obey God, and serving the gracious God we do, we will receive a blessing for our obedience.

How do we apply this principle to our everyday life? How can we change the way we live on a day-to-day basis for God's glory? The answer lies in the appreciation of what God has done. We need to be grateful that the Lord has given us anything at all. We have not earned anything; we have received undeserved gifts only because of His grace. He set up the structure of His economy by creating; then He gave us a commandment to fulfill. If it were not for God doing all of that, we would not even exist, let alone have a purpose.

If you have realized that you are trusting in your own strength rather than God's provisions, take the time right now to ask Him to change your heart. Think about how to honor Him with your blessings rather than using them for selfish ambition.

Prayer of Change

Lord God, thank you for all you have given me. I appreciate you, Jesus. Change my heart so I know what I have comes from you. I ask for wisdom to manage my things for your honor, Lord. Thank you for providing for my needs even when I doubt you. Help me learn more about how your economy works, instead of trusting in the world's systems. In Jesus' name. Amen.

**Economic Principle:
God governs how He chooses and we have the
freedom to choose whether we will follow.**

The LORD God took the man and put him in the garden to work it and take care of it. And the LORD commanded the man, "You are free to eat from any tree in the garden; but you must not eat from the tree of knowledge of good

*and evil, for when you eat of it you will surely die." The
LORD God said, "It is not good for the man to be alone. I
will make a helper suitable for him." Genesis 2:15-18*

*"For this reason a man will leave his father and mother
and be united to his wife, and they will become one
flesh." Genesis 2:24*

Here is the economic lesson: God gives man work to do,
limited by what He wants and desires. Why? Because
that is the way God decided it should be. No other reason is
necessary. He makes the rules. God does not have to explain
any "why" to us.

Later in the book, marriage will be more fully discussed in
terms of financial concepts, but for now, it is important to note
that God specifically says for a man to leave his parents and be
united with his wife. Wives should do the same. The relationship in marriage is a bond that should never be broken.

Marriage is like a garden that needs tending on a regular
basis. We need to work at it in order to enjoy it. When we look
at this economic principle, we see that God gives us something
to do with the blessing He created for us to enjoy. However,
boundaries are involved, and crossing those boundaries entail
consequences. We make choices everyday. Some have good
consequences, others bad.

Genesis chapter 3 discusses the consequences of Adam and
Eve's sin. God does not control us like robots; He gives us freedom to decide what we will do with the economic and material gifts He has provided us. This is His system of dealing with
human beings. This is His economy. We know there is also an
enemy, one that would like to deceive us. In Genesis 3:4 Satan
claims the opposite of what God says will happen: "You will

not surely die," and in the next verse "you will be like God." These two claims are deceptive lies.

Not only are there repercussions for the choices we make, but there is also an enemy seeking whom he may tempt away. We can take this biblical concept one step further by applying it to our financial lives. Ask yourself these questions:

- Why am I spending money in this particular area?
- What do I hope to gain by purchasing this?
- Am I administering my money according to where the Lord would like it to go?
- Is this purchase a need or a fleeting pleasure?

People land themselves in heavy debt because of these issues. Overspending and buying things we cannot afford is a sinful situation and painful consequences ensue. (We have all heard of stress, haven't we?)

Some consequences from this lack of admonishing God's economy include high interest rates and debt repayment. In extreme circumstances, payments to creditors go only to interest and do not reduce the actual debt balance. God gives us another opportunity, however. What we do with that opportunity speaks volumes about our hearts and lifestyle.

So far, we have been introduced to God's economy. He desires us to choose the right things but will let us make our decisions freely. We also know there is an enemy who makes that decision process more troublesome. The Christian life suddenly got a lot more difficult, didn't it?

Life is a series of choices. When you are handling God's resources, remember that your security and value isn't in what you wear or how you look, but in Jesus Christ. Many times we make purchasing decisions based on filling a void we feel. We believe that what we are buying will make us feel better about ourselves. Medication for aliments can come in many forms—pills, overeating, overspending, and so on. Don't give heed to the lie the devil feeds us, "Wow, you look so much better in this expensive suit driving your new Mercedes." Owning an expensive suit or a Mercedes is not a sin; it is using those things to fill the emptiness that only Jesus can fill that pushes God out and establishes an idol in our life.

The goal is to focus on "needs only" buying and the understanding of our identity in Christ. The choices we make display what is in our heart. Whether we are secure in Christ is directly related to our use (or misuse) of money. This inner belief system affects each person in his financial decision-making. As each day dawns, let's make a concentrated effort to ask ourselves if what we are buying is truly needed and is in line with biblical principles.

Prayer of Change

Father God, thank you for this lesson. Help me to remember the consequences of my choices, to follow and obey your Word. Please give me the wisdom to understand and the faith to trust you for my deepest needs. When I use the money and resources you have given me, help me to use them wisely with the purpose of bringing you glory. Thank you, Father God, for forgiving me when I do wrong. I am sorry for the times I have misused your resources for things that did not honor you. My security and self-esteem are grounded in you, Lord, not in anything I can buy. I submit the handling of my money, talents, and time to you, Jesus. I do this out of obedience to you, gracious heavenly Father. In Jesus' name. Amen.

Bribery

Economic Principle: stealing God's glory.

The king of Sodom said to Abram, "Give me the people and keep the goods for yourself." But Abram said to the king of Sodom, "I have raised my hand to the LORD, God Most High, Creator of heaven and earth, and have taken an oath that I will accept nothing belonging to you, not even a thread or the thong or sandal, so that you will never be able to say, 'I made Abram rich.' I will accept nothing but what my men have eaten and the share that belongs to the men who went with me to Aner, Eschol, and Mamre. Let them have their share."
Genesis 14: 21-24

On an earlier raid near the wealthy city of Sodom, Abram's relative Lot and many other people were held captive by nearby kings. Abram and his men rescued Lot and the others and returned to Sodom with the stolen goods, but Abram would not do what the king of Sodom had asked him.

In verse 20, notice that Abram paid a tithe of ten percent upon returning from his victorious mission. As a tribute to God, recognizing He was the reason for the victory, he offered up the best of his spoils. Abram would not violate his oath with God by accepting a bribe from the king of Sodom, nor did he go on his mission for the king out of obedience for God. He did not want there to be any talk among the people that he was receiving payment from the king. Abram wanted God to get all the credit.

This principle of God's economy might be difficult to understand, but it is important to know that we also sometimes need to reject a bribe, however persuasive or enticing it may be. We do not want to be guilty of stealing God's glory or watering down His integrity. Abram did not want to be indebted to the king in any way. How and where we get our resources is directly related to displaying God in our lives. It is easier to stand firm and not be easily swayed when we have our position in mind before the situation arises. For example, if we decide ahead of time that we will not accept bribes from anyone, no matter the situation, when we are offered a new job with better benefits at the cost of sacrificing family time, it will be much easier to turn down. We will not be caught off guard and will honor Christ in our decision.

Situations will inevitable arise in our work and family that we must have conclusions on before we can properly respond. What do we want to display, and what is the ultimate purpose we are trying to achieve? How we make money and acquire assets is important to God. Abram had integrity. So, too, must we. If you face a situation in which you could become rich, but the Holy Spirit has placed unrest in your heart, pray! Seek counsel on these matters *before* making a decision. Wealth can be a hindrance in our walk with the Lord. More "things" is not always best for us; they feed our egos but do not alleviate our spiritual hunger. That does not mean that the more we have, the less spiritual we are. We just need to be sure that God occupies the number one spot in our lives.

Prayer of Change

Almighty God, help me to imitate the example of Abram, to tithe the firstfruits of my possessions faithfully, and to honor and glorify you. Let there be no question about how and where I receive my resources, Lord. They surely come from you. Let everyone see that there is no boasting on my part, but only a humble and thankful attitude about what I have because of your generosity and kindness. Thank you, heavenly Father, in Jesus' name. Amen.

Economic Principle:
bribery is dishonest gain.

The king said to the man of God, "Come home with me and have something to eat, and I will give you a gift." But the man of God answered the king, "Even if you were to give me half your possessions, I would not go with you, nor would I eat bread or drink water here." 1 Kings 13: 7-8

Ahaz took the silver and gold that was found in the house of the LORD and in the treasuries of the king's house, and sent a present to the king of Assyria. 2 Kings 16:8

You shall not distort justice; you shall not be partial, and you shall not take a bribe, for a bribe blinds the eyes of the wise and perverts the words of the righteous. Deuteronomy 16:19

The LORD your God is the God of gods, and the Lord of lords, the great, the mighty, and the awesome God who does not show partiality nor take a bribe. Deuteronomy 10:17

Cursed is he who accepts a bribe to strike down an innocent person. Deuteronomy 27:25

You shall not take a bribe, for a bribe blinds the clear sighted and subverts the cause of the just. Exodus 23:8

The economic lesson presented here is on bribery which is discussed in a variety of circumstances throughout Scripture because the Lord knows that bribes work. People from the beginning of time have used bribes to kill, betray, steal, hurt, destroy, advance politically, gain respect, and every other wicked motive the heart can dream of.

Being involved in a bribe is a sin. To give or receive them is a violation of God's command. In Amos 5:12 the Lord explains, "I know your transgressions are many and your sins are great, you who distress the righteous and accept bribes, and turn aside the poor in the gate."

Bribery comes in many forms besides money: sex, flattery, inappropriate gifts, promotions, raises, false testimony, favors, better treatment in front of others, political games, etc. Bribery grabs hold of our weak spots and uses them to manipulate others. God will not tolerate this behavior in His economy.

Take Inventory of Our Motives

How do we recognize if we are involved in a bribe? First, we must take inventory of our motives in this area. Are our goals blind-sighting us? Have we placed so much emphasis on advancement that we will do whatever it takes to get there? Desires can have such a tenacious hold on our actions that we turn into master manipulators without even realizing it!

You may be working for a company where the prospects for a promotion are nearly non-existent so you begin conspiring how you can get ahead. You realize that the corporate world is not about *what* you know but *who* you know, and you decide that sucking up to your boss and brownnosing the CEO is the best way to get what a promotions. This strategy might work in the world today—in fact, it does—but we as Christians live by a different set of rules. However harmless we make it out to be in our head, it is still a nauseating sin in the eyes of God.

Perhaps you are accepting payment for a job "under the table" or gaining the "inside scoop" through special donations or political transactions. Either way, God does not want "yes men" in His economy, whether we work at 7-11 or Microsoft. If you are a child of God, this is an unacceptable practice.

Approach God in Humility

Secondly, we need to approach the Lord with a humble spirit and ask Him to bring any areas to light that need to be repented of. Through prayer and the infallible Word of God, we can make beneficial decisions. Let's not mess with the plan God has for us, even if the world's way of doing things looks easier. One day, everything hidden will be exposed and none of us want to stand before the judgment seat with chains of bribery hanging off of us like Jacob Marley. We will be blessed for avoiding this perversion.

Prayer of Change

Almighty God, I see how the area of bribery is so prevalent today. Lord, if I have participated in any form of this dark evil, I confess it and repent of it. I want to achieve my goals through honesty and integrity. Help me resist the temptation to accept bribes. I want to have a pure and blameless heart before you. I pray this in Jesus' name. Amen.

TALKING BACK TO GOD

Economic Principle: testing God's patience.

The Israelites were fruitful and multiplied greatly and became exceedingly numerous, so that the land was filled with them. Then a new king, who did not know about Joseph, came to power in Egypt. "Look," he said to his people, "the Israelites have become much too numerous for us. Come, we must deal shrewdly with them or they will become even more numerous and, if war breaks out, will join our enemies, fight against us, and leave the country." So they put slave masters over them to oppress them with forced labor, and they built Pithom and Rameses as store cities for Pharaoh. But the more they were oppressed, the more they multiplied and spread; so the Egyptians came to dread the Israelites and worked them ruthlessly." Exodus 1:7-13

God heard their groaning and he remembered his covenant with Abraham, with Isaac and with Jacob. So God looked on the Israelites and was concerned about them. Exodus 2:24-25

So I have come down to rescue them from the hand of the Egyptians, and to bring them up out of that land into a good and spacious land, a land flowing with milk and honey. Exodus 3:8

Moses said to the LORD, *"O Lord, I have never been eloquent, neither in the past nor since you have spoken to*

*your servant. I am slow of speech and tongue." The
LORD said to him, "Who gave man his mouth? Who
makes him deaf or mute? Who gives him sight or makes
him blind? Is it not I the LORD? Now go; I will help you
speak and will teach you what to say." But Moses said,
"O Lord, please send someone else to do it." Then the
LORD's anger burned against Moses and He said, "What
about your brother, Aaron the Levite? I know he can
speak well. He is already on his way to meet you, and
his heart will be glad when he sees you."* Exodus 4:10-14

Moses had everything he needed for a comfortable lifestyle: a job, a family, nice weather, and a good place to live. But he had some serious character flaws, just like the rest of us. He was disrespectful, sparring with God and trying to "sell" Him on finding someone else. God will always equip us for what He has called us to do. He keeps His promises; it is humans who break their word. God wanted to use Moses in a dramatic way, but he was unwilling to step out in faith.

You put yourself in a dangerous position when you test God's patience. No one will ever succeed in frustrating His sovereign plan. He is a compassionate and loving God, but He is also just and He punishes all wrongdoing.

How do we change the way we live from now on based on these economic principles? In your own walk with Christ, how often have you argued with God about something the Holy Spirit has put on your heart? Hasn't God been exceedingly patient with us? Of course He has. That is one of His great attributes, but let us not test His patience. He commands; we obey.

As we live each day, let's turn an ear to that still small voice we feel prompting us. Listening is not the hard part; anyone with an ear can do that. It is applying what we hear to our life that is more difficult. But like everything else, it becomes easier with practice and from reading the Scriptures and applying them to our everyday life. James 1:22 (NIV) says, "Do not merely listen to the word, and so deceive yourselves. Do what it says."

Real wisdom is tangibly applying biblical truths we know to our everyday life. This is when the rubber hits the road. There will inevitably be days when we just want to throw in the towel, but God uses these opportunities to mature us in our faith in Him. Be faithful to God. He knows exactly what difficulty or hardship we are experiencing. The important thing is to do what is right in His eyes.

Prayer of Change

Lord God, thank you for this lesson. Help me to learn and do what you teach. I do not want to talk back to you or try to outfox you in my heart. Help me to look for the opportunities you give me to practice your truths. Thank you for your mercies and patience with me. Without you I am nothing. Change my attitude, Lord, to be compliant and kind towards you and others. In Jesus' name. Amen.

Covetousness

Economic Principle:
creating an idol through greedy thoughts.

And God spoke all these words: "I am the Lord *your God, who brought you out of Egypt, out of the land of slavery. You shall have no other gods before me. You shall not make for yourself an idol in the form of anything in heaven above or beyond the earth beneath or in the waters below. You shall not bow down to them or worship them; for I the* Lord *your God am a jealous God, punishing the children for the sins of their fathers to the third and fourth generation of those who hate me, but showing love to a thousand generations of those who love me and keep my commandments. You shall not misuse the name of the Lord your God, for the* Lord *will not hold anyone guiltless who misuses his name. Remember the Sabbath day by keeping it holy. Six days you shall labor and do all your work, but the seventh day is a Sabbath to the* Lord *your God. On it, you shall not do any work, neither you, nor your son or daughter, nor your manservant or maidservant, nor your animals, nor the aliens within your gates. For in six days the* Lord *made the heavens and the earth, the sea, and all that is in them, but he rested on the seventh day. Therefore the* Lord *blessed the Sabbath day and made it holy. Honor your father and your mother, so that you may live long in the land the* Lord *your God is giving you. You shall not murder. You shall not commit adultery. You shall not steal. You shall not give false testimony against your neighbor. You shall not covet your neighbor's house. You shall not covet your neighbor's wife, or his manservant or maidservant, his ox or donkey, or anything that belongs to your neighbor."* Exodus 20:1-17

Remember that God's economy works differently than anything a person or government could create. No system created by man or any culture he has established operates like God's system. His ways are not our ways. His thoughts are not our thoughts (see Isaiah 55:8). But by doing what God says to do, we will be blessed in numerous ways. These blessings may not come in monetary form, but we will receive them as promised.

A major lesson can be learned concerning envy and jealousy. As a financial counselor and adviser, many people I work with make financial mistakes because of envy and jealousy. What starts in the heart snowballs into long-lasting problems, many of which manifest themselves financially. The simplest and most common problem is the need we feel to "keep up with the Joneses." The dictionary defines jealousy as "being disposed to suspect rivalry or unfaithfulness." Envy is defined as "malice, to begrudge someone, or painful or resentful awareness of an advantage enjoyed by another joined with the desire to possess the same advantage." One of the deep reasons for Cain murdering Abel was envy. Because Abel's offering was acceptable and Cain's was not, he resented Abel and envied his reward from God.

God is not opposed to His children owning things, experiencing wealth, or possessing assets. However, He is opposed to their becoming covetous. We see in the economy of God that He is not a bully or mean cosmic potentate, but He is concerned about the false gods that ensue when we put too much emphasis on "things." The heart is where the seed is planted, where we begin to resent that we do not have a fair share or being discontented with what we have. Some people can never have enough and they end up in financial bondage. We see something someone else has and we want it! The life of a Christian should not be characterized by selfishness, greed, or envy. The dictionary defines covetousness as "having a craving for possession, to wish for enviously, or an inordinate desire for what belongs to another."

Ephesians 5:5 says, "This you know with certainty, that no immoral or impure person or covetous man, who is an idolater, has an inheritance in the kingdom of Christ and God."

When we envy someone, we create an idol. That puts something deep and desirous in our heart before God who should always occupy the number one slot in our life. First Peter 2:1 says to put "aside all malice and all deceit and hypocrisy and envy and all slander." A way we can do this is to apply Proverbs 23:17, "Do not let your heart envy sinners, but live in the fear of the LORD always."

In Exodus 20:6, we read that if we love God, we will keep His commandments. That truth is supported throughout the Bible. In God's economy we prove whether or not we love Him by our desire to obey His commandments. In the New Testament, one of the Pharisees asked Jesus which of the commandments was the most important. Jesus answered. "Hear, O Israel, the Lord our God, the Lord is one. Love the Lord your God with all your heart and with all your soul and with all your mind and with all your strength. The second is this: Love your neighbor as yourself. There is no commandment greater than these" (Mark 12:29-31).

In order to love God, we need to obey the commandments He has given. How appreciative of God's grace I am! I take inventory of my heart and think about my walk with Christ, only to see that I fall far short of the mark. Take inventory of your heart, fellow brother or sister.

Here is where the rubber meets the road and we must apply the lessons to our life. We must live without envy and covetousness. Look at your spending records, budgets, check registers, and credit card statements. Be honest and open. Why have you spent what you have spent? Review your motives, see if the purchases had envious roots. Examine in depth why you bought something. Even if you did not have to go into debt to buy it, was it a worthwhile purchase? Did it fill a temporary void, or has it satisfied a true need?

Look at your financial goals and objectives. What are your goals? Do you have any financial aspirations for the near future? How about long term? If you do not have any current goals, we will explain how to establish them later in the book. For now, keep the following ideas in mind.

Everything we do in the economic realm, and the moral realm for that matter, has a motive behind it. Proverbs 16:2 says, "All a man's ways seem innocent to him, but motives are weighed by the LORD."

We can appreciate what our neighbor has, drives, and who he is married to, but it is a sin to envy it for our self. Many times envy rears its ugly head due to an issue we have with self-esteem. This is because deep down we do not believe that the Lord can fill the emptiness we feel. Do you hear the rotten voice of Satan in your head saying, "If you had that, you would be a lot more successful," or "You loser, when will you amount to anything"? Shut that voice out. Do not listen to it! It will only lead you further down a miserable road.

There will be many temptations thrown at us on our walk through life, especially as we seek to glorify God. We will want to buy things we cannot afford. We will try to justify the fact that we *need* this certain item when, in reality, we can live fine without it. So let's take a good, hard look at our spending habits, along with our reasons for buying what we do so. Before we write a check, remember that a motive has already been forming…is it a pure one?

Do not forget that there is a blessing from re-thinking our financial motivations. Heading down the right road brings us closer to financial peace and freedom. Financial bondage brings stress which leads to grouchiness, reservation, and a tangled mess of neglected relationships. The high road is simply one of obedience in which the Lord will be pleased and we will be blessed. Recite this saying when feeding unhealthy self-esteem issues: *Financial net worth does not equal personal self-worth.*

Prayer of Change

Lord, show me what is taking place in my heart as I manage the resources you have given me. Help me to obey you, God, in all ten of the commandments. Help me not to envy others, but instead to be happy for their success. Teach me to be filled with your truth and contentment, for in that I lack nothing. Father in heaven, work in me to be like Jesus. Give me the determination to say "no" to things I really do not need. Thank you for your provision and wisdom. In Jesus' name. Amen.

RESTITUTION

Economic Principle: restoring what was taken.

*The LORD said to Moses, "If anyone sins and is unfaith-
ful to the LORD by deceiving his neighbor about something entrusted to him or left in his care or stolen, or if
he cheats him, or if he finds lost property and lies about
it, or if he swears falsely, or if he commits any such sin
that people may do—when he thus sins and becomes
guilty, he must return what he has stolen or taken by
extortion, or what was entrusted to him, or the lost
property he found, or whatever it was he swore falsely
about. He must make restitution in full, add a fifth of
the value to it and give it all to the owner on the day he
gives his guilt offering."* Leviticus 6:1-5

*Zaccheus stopped and said to the Lord, "Behold, Lord,
half of my possessions I will give to the poor, and if I
have defrauded anyone of anything, I will give back four
times as much." And Jesus said to him, "Today salvation
has come to this house, because he, too, is a son of
Abraham."* Luke 19:8-9

The economic principle here is restitution. Restitution is
defined in Webster's dictionary as "an act of restoring or
a condition of being restored to the rightful owner."

If the Holy Spirit is living inside of us, we are not going to
be able to enjoy ill-gotten fruits. That unrest in our hearts is
evidence that our conscience has not gone numb. As a result of
this prompting, we are to repay what we have cheated, plus

extra. This is a "pain and suffering" reimbursement for the person who endured harm. Zaccheus repaid 400 percent, and we, too, should go the extra mile to make things right.

In God's economy we need to say we are sorry and ask forgiveness of the offended party. We need to reconcile with people just as we do with God when we sin. First we confess, then we repent, and lastly, we ask for forgiveness. This principle teaches us to go one step further and restore what was lost. Not only must we restore, but we must also reconcile. For example, if we use a coworker's supplies without asking and he gets upset, God's economy shows us that we need to replace what we used and then patch up the relationship with our coworker.

Matthew 5:23-24 speaks of reconciliation: "Therefore, if you are offering your gift at the altar and there remember that your brother has something against you, leave your gift in front of the altar. First go and be reconciled to your brother, then come and offer your gift."

Avoiding confrontation or hiding from someone is not God's way of solving a problem. Avoidance does not bring healing or victory; it only prolongs the uncomfortable situation. Restoring relationships and repaying what is owed brings peace to our hearts. No more sleepless nights or agonizing confrontations, just quiet joy. If you have any outstanding debts with anyone, confess and repent today. Put things back in God's proper order and learn from your mistake.

Prayer of Change

Father God, help me to learn the way of restoration in money, property, and relationships. Lord, teach me why and how it happened so I do not repeat the same situation. Help me to value relationships more than whatever else I am trying to gain. Allow me to pay back in full anyone I have wronged. Grant me grace to forgive those who owe me. You demonstrated your love on the cross when I least deserved it. Help me to imitate that model. In Jesus' name. Amen.

ARROGANCE

Economic Principle:
creating an idol through self-image.

When you have eaten and are satisfied, praise the LORD your God for the good land he has given you. Be careful that you do not forget the LORD your God, failing to observe his commands, his laws and his decrees that I am giving you this day. Otherwise, when you eat and are satisfied, when you build fine houses and settle down, and when your herds and flocks grow large and your silver and gold increase and all you have is multiplied, then your heart will become proud and you will forget the LORD your God, who brought you out of Egypt, out of the land of slavery. He led you through the vast and dreadful desert, that thirsty and waterless land, with its venomous snakes and scorpions. He brought you water out of hard rock. He gave you manna to eat in the desert, something your fathers had never known, to humble and to test you so that in the end it might go well with you. You may say to yourself, "My power and the strength of my hands have produced this wealth for me." But remember the LORD your God, for it is he that gives you the ability to produce wealth, and so confirms his covenant, which he swore to your forefathers, as it is today. If you ever forget the LORD your God and follow other gods and worship and bow down to them, I testify against you today that you will surely be destroyed. Like the nations the LORD destroyed before you, so you will be destroyed for not obeying the LORD your God. Deuteronomy 8:10-20

The Lord has a valid concern for us: He knows that prosperity can lead to pride. Arrogance is the sin that cast Satan out of heaven, and arrogance can make Christians backslide into the muck and mire. A haughty spirit places one's own self above God, thus creating an idol and breaking the first commandment.

Prosperity can easily cause a prideful perspective in us as well. We think thoughts of how great we are, and if it were not for our own ambition, we would not be where we are. Then it is only a short time before God is on the back burner, simmering with jealousy.

As believers, with hearts focused on bringing God glory, we need to avoid anything that creates a wall between the Lord and us. Proverbs 16:18 says that "pride goes before destruction, and a haughty spirit before stumbling." Allowing arrogance to grow in our hearts is setting us up for disaster!

So how can we fix this problem, or better yet, stop it before it starts? Proverbs 16:19 states, "It is better to be humble in spirit with the lowly than to divide the spoil with the proud." Do not bite the enemy's hook, but remember that God is the one who blesses and keeps you. He granted that promotion; He allowed an inheritance to come through. Our self-esteem cannot be wrapped up in our job titles or assets, but only in the security of knowing Christ as our Savior. Contrary to popular opinion material achievements do not elevate us; obedience to God does.

"Everyone who is proud in heart is an abomination to the LORD; assuredly, he will not go unpunished" (Proverbs 16:5). Do you believe this verse? It may sound harsh, but it is true. God did not create us only to cast us to hell, We are His craftsmanship. Let's live like it!

Having riches is not evil, but prizing them is. If we are using the Lord's money He has so generously bestowed upon us to further our own personal success, our priorities are seriously out of whack; we are in danger of a rude awakening. However, if we are using what we have to further the gospel and fulfill the Great Commission, treasures will pile up for us in heaven. Which would you rather experience?

Prayer of Change

Lord God, help me to always remember the scripture in Deuteronomy. I know in my mind and believe in my heart that you gave me everything I have. You provide for my needs, not my prideful ego. Lord, I confess and repent of when I have had a prideful spirit. The blessings in the good times are from you, as are the lessons I learn in the hard times. Help me to live with the knowledge and understanding that you are the Supplier. Let me not forget that in abundance or want, you are by my side. Use my material possessions for your glory. In Jesus' name. Amen.

GOD AS PROVIDER

Economic Principle:
trusting through the hard times.
Ruth 1–4

This is a story about two rather common people with extraordinary qualities. These two ladies had endured unheard-of hardship after their husbands and sons died while a famine riveted the land. Their futures looked extremely bleak.

Although they might not have known where their next meal was coming from, they trusted God for provisions. They did not give up during even the most intense struggle. Ruth promised her undying devotion to her mother-in-law Naomi when she did not have to. She had absolutely no obligation to Naomi, but she witnessed Naomi's trust in God's sovereign plan.

God was in complete control of Naomi and Ruth's situation. Ruth was not ashamed to go gleaning in someone else's field; she knew she had to use the hands the Lord had given her to make a living. As a result of her perseverance, the Lord used Boaz to bless her. He provided her with food, a home, and a child who would be the grandfather of King David! Nothing could be a more incredible ending to a bitter beginning. This is what God is in the business of doing: taking broken lives and piecing them into a beautifully intricate puzzle.

God also has a plan for us, just as He did for Ruth and Naomi. Jeremiah 29:11-13 says, " 'For I know the plans I have for you," declares the LORD, 'plans to prosper you and not to harm you, plans to give you hope and a future. Then you will call upon me and come and pray to me, and I will listen to you. You will seek me and find me when you seek me with all your heart.' "

Pain occurs in life, sometimes through the death of a spouse or betrayal of a loved one. A lack of adequate money flow added to that equation leads to a large amount of stress. But God calls for faithfulness in the midst of suffering. Two things He does not want are complaining and a bitter spirit. He can do little with a person unwilling to trust Him and wallowing in misery. Instead, we should be diligent workers, pouring our hearts out to God.

Ladies, there is a valuable lesson to be learned here from Ruth's character as a woman of God. She persevered, was loyal, worked with her hands, exhibited a humble spirit, and honored the man in her life. Proverbs 31 says, "A wife of noble character who can find? She is worth far more than rubies...She is clothed with strength and dignity; she can laugh at the days to come. She speaks with wisdom, and faithful instruction is on her tongue" (10-11, 24-25). Ladies, strive to be like Ruth and the Proverbs 31 woman. Gentlemen, encourage your wives, or if you are single, look for a woman with these godly attributes.

Prayer of Change

Father God, thank you for this great lesson from Ruth. In the midst of struggling or tragedy, help me to trust you and love you while thinking of the needs of others as well. Help me to be dedicated to you as I work for a living. Lord, bring me opportunities for ministry among my neighbors and people I work with or know are in need of encouragement. Please work in my attitudes and emotions. Give me sensitivity for widows and the needy. I want to be a witness and tool for you. In Jesus' name I pray. Amen.

USURY

Economic Principle:
taking advantage of the poor.

The wife of a man from the company of the prophets cried out to Elisha, "Your servant my husband is dead, and you know that he revered the LORD. But now his creditor is coming to take my two boys as his slaves." Elisha replied to her, "How can I help you? Tell me, what do you have in your house?" "Your servant has nothing there at all," she said, "except a little oil." Elisha said, "Go around and ask all your neighbors for empty jars. Don't ask for just a few. Then go inside and shut the door behind you and your sons. Pour oil into all the jars, and as each is filled, put it to one side." She left him and afterward shut the door behind her and her sons. They brought the jars to her and she kept pouring. When all the jars were full, she said to her son, "Bring me another one." But he replied, "There is not a jar left." Then the oil stopped flowing. She went and told the man of God, and he said to her, "Go, sell the oil and pay your debts. You and your sons can live on what is left." 2 Kings 4:1-7

This is the story of a widow with great faith. She lost her husband, but not all the debts he owed. In ancient times, if a person could not pay his debts, he was sold into slavery until he worked them off. This is also known as usury. The Lord does not approve of unfair usury laws because they take advantage of the poor. A poor man is at the mercy of the loan shark who establishes the exorbitant rates and decides how he wants to be repaid.

God is completely opposed to this economic manipulation. But as we read on in this passage, we understand that God rescues His followers and provides for their needs. The economic lesson to be learned here is that the Lord is our sustainer. He sustained the widow and her sons in a miraculous way! They did not have any food stamps or welfare checks to fall back on, but they did have a prophet who spoke the words of God. The widow sought advice and then applied it to her life. She desperately wanted to protect her family from the vicious creditors she feared would exploit them. God met her need and gave her an extra provision to live on.

This story illustrates to us that in uncertain and scary times we must lean on God. We do not have a wise prophet to talk to, but we do have a relationship with the omniscient God of the universe who has given us everything we need for life and godliness in His Word. We must be careful from whom and where we seek our answers. Ask the Lord first, and then search for wise counsel. Do not heed the advice of your hairstylist if it is only what *you* want to hear. He or she may have a beneficial admonishment, but if it does not match up with the Word of God, do not listen to it.

We are on a spiritual journey. We may not have neon lights flashing God's will at us, but all abiding Christians are on a quest, without exception. God is looking to make us more Christ-like and spiritually mature. He wants to draw us closer into fellowship and faith in Him through Jesus Christ.

One way we learn to trust Jesus more completely is through trials. Suffering brings us to a point of utter dependence on God because we cannot change our circumstances ourselves. James 1:2-4 says, "Consider it pure joy, my brothers, whenever you face trials of many kinds, because you know that the testing of your faith develops perseverance. Perseverance must finish its work so that you may be mature and complete, not lacking anything."

Struggling through the hard times will make us stronger just as exercising at the gym builds up our muscles over time. Tribulations are like our spiritual bench presses! And look at the reward we will receive for pressing on. "Blessed is the man who perseveres under trial, because when he has stood the test, he will receive the crown of life which God has promised to those who love him" (James 1:12).

When we seek the Lord for His guidance and answers, sometimes He responds in ways we do not expect. A prayer for more money seems like a logical plea for a tight financial situation, but God may want us to struggle awhile because He sees a better opportunity down the road. "No" may not be the response we desire, but it is the right answer for sustaining and keeping us on the path Christ has for us. Remember the promise of Jeremiah 29:11 we mentioned earlier. God works everything out for His glory and our best. Trust Him on that.

Prayer of Change

Lord, like the widow in 2 Kings, help me to seek you in times of trouble. Help me to pray for those who might intend harm for me, or who may take advantage of me in a dire situation. Lord, advise me and counsel me. Help me to listen to you and follow through without complaint, whatever you may direct. Help me to follow your economic principles and change the way I live on a daily basis.

Only you know the truth, Lord, and in my journey, help me to see and do what you teach me from your

Word. I do not want to be swayed by man's philoso-
phies, so help me to value the authority of your Word
above all. In Jesus' name. Amen.

Economic Principle:
economic manipulation using people.

Now the men and their wives raised a great outcry
against their Jewish brothers. Some were saying, "We
and our sons and daughters are numerous; in order for
us to eat and stay alive, we must get grain." Others were
saying, "We are mortgaging our fields, our vineyards
and our homes to get grain during the famine." Still
others were saying, "We have had to borrow money to
pay the king's tax on our fields and vineyards. Although
we are of the same flesh and blood as our countrymen
and though our sons are as good as theirs, yet we have
to subject our sons and daughters to slavery. Some of
our daughters have already been enslaved, but we are
powerless, because our fields and our vineyards belong
to others."
When I heard their outcry and these charges, I was very
angry. I pondered them in my mind and then accused
the nobles and officials. I told them, "You are exacting
usury from your own countrymen!" So I called together
a large meeting to deal with them and said: "As far as
possible, we have bought back our Jewish brothers who
were sold to the Gentiles. Now you are selling your
brothers, only for them to be sold back to us!" They kept
quiet because they could find nothing to say. So I con-
tinued, "What you are doing is not right. Should not

you walk in the fear of our God to avoid the reproach of our Gentile enemies? I and my brothers and my men are also lending the people money and grain. But let the exacting of usury stop! Give back to them immediately their fields, vineyards, olive groves and houses, and also the usury you are charging them—the hundredth part of the money, grain, new wine and oil."

"We will give it back," they said. "And we will not demand anything more from them. We will do as you say." Then I summoned the priests and made the nobles and officials take an oath to do what they had promised. I also shook out the folds of my robe and said, "In this way may God shake out of his house and possessions every man who does not keep this promise. So may such a man be shaken out and emptied!"

At this the whole assembly said, "Amen," and praised the LORD. And the people did as they had promised. Moreover, from the twentieth year of King Artaxerxes, when I was appointed to be their governor in the land of Judah, until his thirty-second year—twelve years—neither I nor my brothers ate the food allotted to the governor. But the earlier governors—those preceding me—placed a heavy burden on the people and took forty shekels of silver from them in addition to food and wine. Their assistants also lorded it over the people. But out of reverence for God I did not act like that. Instead, I devoted myself to the work on this wall. All my men were assembled there for the work; we did not acquire any land.

Furthermore, a hundred and fifty Jews and officials ate at my table, as well as those who came to us from surrounding nations. Each day one ox, six choice sheep,

and some poultry were prepared for me, and every ten
days an abundant supply of wine of all kinds. In spite of
all this, I never demanded the food allotted to the gover-
nor, because the demands were heavy on these people.
Remember me with favor, O my God, for all I have
done for these people. Nehemiah 5:1-19

Along with external opposition that was affecting Nehemiah
and the completion of the wall, there were serious inter-
nal problems as well. Nehemiah was trying to rebuild the city
and the people within the walls were crumbling to pieces
because of dissension caused by usury.

The Jews were charging exorbitant interest rates to their fellow brethren. In addition, the Persians were also levying a heavy
tax. Greed was rampant back then just as it is today. And, similar to now, people were mortgaging their land and homes to pay
their expenses and Jews were selling their own children into
slavery. Throughout history, the upper class has lorded their
lofty position over the poor for the prize of money.

This was the economy Nehemiah was faced with—in stark
contrast with the economy God desired. As long as we have sin
in this world—which will be until Jesus comes back—
exploitation will always be a way people make money.

Webster's dictionary says usury is "interest in excess of a
legal rate charged to a borrower for the use of money." Those
who practice exploitation will ultimately reap their ruin as
shown in Proverbs 28:8: "He who increases his wealth by interest and usury, gathers it for him who is gracious to the poor."
At least we can be assured that their evil act will not go unpunished. Nehemiah took action when he confronted the Jews. He
told them that they were reproaching the name of God and living in sin.

As a counteraction, Nehemiah organized everyone and had them make an oath to stop their evil acts. He promised consequences to anyone who disobeyed. Praise the Lord; it worked.

Out of respect for God, Nehemiah decided that he would not add to his income by creating another tax. Wanting to be an authority figure that set an example, he chose to take the road of integrity.

God wants us to apply this lesson to our lives and be like Nehemiah. We should never charge anyone an amount they would never be able to repay. Just as is characteristic of the Lord, we need to demonstrate compassion and mercy. If you are guilty of usury, you can begin today to make it right by applying all overcharged interest to the original debt and creating new, reasonable terms. If you are experiencing mistreatment in this way, go to the person and share these passages in hope of helping him understand God's economy.

Prayer of Change

Lord, help me to be like Nehemiah and have other people's interests at heart. Steer me away from the temptation to demand more than I deserve. Holy Spirit, hold me accountable by keeping me sensitive to your Word and promptings. Help me learn this lesson in a practical way. In Jesus' name. Amen.

THE LORD GIVES AND TAKES AWAY

Economic Principle:
trials develop character.

The LORD gave and the LORD has taken away; may the name of the LORD be praised. Job 1:21

His wife said to him, "Are you still holding on to your integrity? Curse God and die!" He replied, "You are talking like a foolish woman. Shall we accept good from God, and not trouble?" In all this, Job did not sin in what he said. Job 2:9-10

The economic principles that come from the book of Job are numerous, but they can be broken down into some major themes. For example, sometimes in life we experience great losses, and yet we should still praise God. Job was a man just like us, capable of making decisions and experiencing pain. He lost everything, even his own health, but he never cursed God. We have no guarantees in this world that our money, health, and families will last. The Lord holds everything in His hands and can take things away whenever He sees fit.

In the midst of all the struggles, the blistering boils on his skin, and his family and friends deserting him, Job continued to praise the Lord. Convinced that the Lord must have a reason behind what He was doing, Job trusted Him. Do we trust the Lord when the world seems to come crashing down?

The second thing we need to learn from Job is that happiness does not come from things going our way all the time. As adults, we know that we cannot have our cake and eat it too.

Our happiness and praise to God should not be dependent on our circumstances. Job had nothing; he did not even have the health of his own body. His wife asked him to curse God, but he knew better. Job was in the midst of the worst suffering endured by man (except for the sufferings of Christ), and still he praised God for His faithfulness and righteousness.

When Job was restored and blessed with double he had before, the Lord had grown his character to the point of being better used for the kingdom. Second Corinthians 1:3-10 shows us how good things can come from evil. Here we see how we are shaped through suffering in order to grow spiritually. In turn, we can comfort and guide others as they experience what we have already learned.

Job did not know how the end would turn out. He was in a tunnel, unable to see the light ahead, but in blindness he trusted God. He stumbled, he questioned God, he spoke foolishness and challenged Him, but he also sought the Lord. He did not check out just because the going got tough.

How do we apply this lesson to our everyday lives, and what blessings can we expect as responding Christians? Without question, we will all go through troubles in our lives, especially financial struggles. It is not a question of *if* it will happen, but *when*. We can try to maneuver our way through life, but sooner or later the trials will hit. Maybe your business will go bankrupt, your stocks will crash, a tax problem will leave you poor, or a hurricane will literally blow away your house. Spouses die and income halts. People are laid off or fired from their jobs. Inevitably these things will happen.

How we handle and respond to these things is the key! Will we be angry with God or draw closer to Him? It is hard to count pain as "joy" as James 1 says, but God loves us with all His heart. This love is made manifest when we see that the

Bible has the answer to all of life's questions. God has already provided a map to guide us through life. We must read it carefully and introspectively.

Our feelings are valid. To deny that would be a lie. We hurt when bad things happen; God made us to function that way. The key is to *tell* the Lord that we are hurting. He wants to be intimately involved with us emotionally. It is okay to cry. Jesus did (see John 17:35).

We must be careful from whom and where we get our advice. Job had friends who saw only a minute piece of the picture and a wife who cursed God. Even in the Christian community we must be careful whom we listen to. Christians can be wrong too. That's why we must always evaluate counsel. If it does not match up with the Word of God, we received bad advice! Do not dishonor the Lord by valuing worldly advice over His Word, no matter how justifiable your situation.

Proverbs 13:20 says, "He who walks with wise men will be wise, but the companion of fools will suffer harm." Proverbs 14:7 reiterates the same idea. "Leave the presence of a fool, or you will not discern words of knowledge." Surround yourself with believing friends so you can trust the majority of what you hear. However, sometimes our ears want to hear certain things and our spirit earnestly wants to believe them so badly, we forget to evaluate the advice next to Scripture. Guard against this.

"There is a way that seems right to a man, but in the end it leads to destruction" (Proverbs 16:25). Some of the storms we experience are brought on by our own disobedience and unwise decisions. So with the promise of Romans 8:28 supporting Him, God uses these "tempests" to lovingly redirect us. "My son, do not reject the discipline of the Lord, or loathe His reproof, for whom the Lord loves He reproves, even as a father corrects the son in whom he delights" (Proverbs 3:11-12).

In summary, so far we see from the book of Job that:

- God can give and take away as He sees fit.
- We can trust the Lord with our circumstances because He is faithful.
- Trouble and suffering are inevitable.
- We must persevere through tragedy, giving God praise continually.
- Sometimes we cause our own problems.
- The Lord lovingly reproves us.

I knew a man who poured all his time, energy, and money into his business. He even mortgaged his house to pay for parts of it. When the business began to fail, so did his marriage. For this man, like so many others, the success of his business was a reflection of his success as a person. When his business failed, he felt absolutely worthless. The man's problem was not in his business skills, but in the fact that he valued them far above anything else.

So why should this man not despair? Simply because God loves him. He finally got to a point where God was his only source of hope. He learned that the formula for security and significance was not based on society's view of his business, but rather in his relationship with his Savior. He re-set his goals, learned time management, embraced contentment rather than dissatisfaction, and began to control his business instead of it controlling him.

At his lowest point he wanted to commit suicide, but through the guidance of his God and loving support of family and friends, he was restored. The encouragement and comfort of his friends not only lifted *this* man's spirit, but also can do the same for anyone. We must be supportive when our loved ones face excruciating trials and reflect the love of God in a positive and tangible way, so they are reminded of God's continual presence in our lives.

Prayer of Change

Lord, thank you for the lessons in Job. Help me learn to love and obey you, even in times of loss and suffering. God, I acknowledge that you have the right to give or take. I trust you to do whatever is necessary to keep me in an abiding relationship with you. I want to learn to praise you no matter the circumstance. Give me faith to trust you, Jesus, even when I do not feel like it or understand why I am going through a trial. My life is in your hands. In Jesus' name I pray. Amen.

Part **2**

GIVING

MOTIVES FOR GIVING

Economic Principle:
The Lord knows the intentions of the heart.

One man gives freely, yet gains even more; another withholds unduly, but comes to poverty. A generous man will prosper; he who refreshes others will himself be refreshed. Proverbs 11:24-25

Be careful not to do your "acts of righteousness" before men, to be seen by them. If you do, you will have no reward from your Father in heaven. So when you give to the needy, do not announce it with trumpets, as the hypocrites do in the synagogues and on the streets, to be honored by men. I tell you the truth, they have received their reward in full. But when you give to the needy, do not let your left hand know what your right hand is doing, so that your giving may be in secret. Then your Father, who sees what is done in secret, will reward you. Matthew 6:1-4

Every man shall give as he is able, according to the blessing of the LORD your God which He has given you. Deuteronomy 16:17

Joseph, a Levite of Cyprian birth, who was also called Barnabas by the apostles (which translated means Son of Encouragement), and who owned a tract of land, sold it and brought money and laid it at the apostles' feet. Acts 4:36-37

*But who am I, and who are my people, that we should
be able to give as generously as this? Everything comes
from you, and we have given you only what comes from
your hand.* 1 Chronicles 29:14

*I know, my God, that you test the heart and are pleased
with integrity. All these things have I given willingly
and with honest intent. And now I have seen with joy
how willingly your people who are here have given to
you.* 1 Chronicles 29:17

*All a man's ways seem innocent to him, but motives are
weighed by the Lord."* Proverbs 16:2

*The congregation of those who believed were of one
heart and soul; and not one of them claimed that anything belonging to him was his own; but all things
were common property to them. And with great power
the apostles were giving witness to the resurrection of
the Lord Jesus, and abundant grace was upon them
all. For there was not a needy person among them, for
all who were owners of land and houses would sell
them and bring the proceeds of the sales and lay them
at the apostles' feet, and they would be distributed to
each as any had need.* Acts 4:32-35

*Instruct them to do good, to be rich in good works, to
be generous and ready to share, storing up for themselves the treasure of a good foundation for the future,
so that they may take hold of that which is life indeed.*
1 Timothy 6:18-19

Whoever has the world's goods, and sees his brother in need and closes his heart against him, how does the love of God abide in him? Little children, let us not love with word or with tongue, but in deed and truth.
1 John 3:17-18

Do not neglect doing good and sharing, for with such sacrifices God is pleased. Hebrews 13:16

And remember the words of the Lord Jesus, that He Himself said, "It is more blessed to give than to receive."
Acts 20:35

If I give all I possess to the poor and surrender my body to the flames, but have not love, I gain nothing.
1 Corinthians 13:3

Before we discuss the different principles about giving and tithing, we need to consider the right and wrong motives for giving. We know that giving can include much more than currency. Too often Christians think just in terms of how much money they are giving, but there are things to give besides cash. In fact, other gifts may be more relevant and meaningful. A visit to an ill person may be more appreciated than a check in the mail. Praying with them has great value as well, and God cannot help but be honored.

Giving can also include donating blood to the Red Cross to help others in a time of emergency or disaster. It might also be giving of our talents musically, creatively, or administratively. Or how about giving someone a ride to church who cannot drive? You can think of other ways to fulfill a need someone has. Here is a list of good motives for giving:

1. Giving out of obedience to Scripture
2. Giving to glorify God
3. Helping others come to know the Lord and be saved
4. Giving to the poor
5. Giving to the needy, and those in prison or hospitals
6. Giving your talents in your church or another ministry
8. Giving so a person might learn how to thank God
9. Giving out of gratitude for what God has already given
10. Giving to learn how to trust God for our needs
11. Giving with a cheerful heart
12. Giving sacrificially
13. Giving secretively or quietly

Here is a list for bad motives of giving:

1. Giving to get
2. Giving to be seen or get attention
3. Giving out of legalism
4. Giving to earn a place in heaven
5. Giving out of obligation or compulsion
6. Giving to gain a place of leadership
7. Giving to gain partiality and favor
8. Giving useless gifts

Here is a list of gifts that can be given:

1. Money and currency
2. Stocks, bonds, and securities
3. Household goods and furniture
4. Talents
5. Time
6. Real estate

7. Appreciated securities
8. Apartments, second homes
9. Collections
10. Jewelry
11. Food, clothing
12. Bibles
13. Blood and organ donations

We cannot and should not hide from opportunities to give, and we must not turn the other way pretending we did not notice the need. If we do, we are denying our responsibility as believers and quenching the work of the Holy Spirit. God's economic principle is clear: He wants us to give hilariously, full of fun and cheerfulness. Giving with an attitude of "What's in it for me?" or out of obligation thwarts the Lord's work through us and prevents us from reaping a blessing. Just because Aunt Martha bought everyone Disneyland passes for Christmas certainly does not warrant a needless spending of cash to try to keep up with her. Let her give, and if her motive is not right, the Lord will deal with it. The lesson to be learned is to give within *your* means and with a happy heart.

Much more can be extracted on the issue of giving. It is an amazing subject in the Bible; that is why we quoted so many verses and there are many more supportive texts we could have added. The amount of words, time, and lessons about generosity in the Scriptures are exhaustive. God devoted so much of His Holy Word to the subject for a reason—He wants us to understand this attribute of His character. He is the ultimate Giver. He does not ever ask Himself, "What will I get out of this?" or "What if this investment does not pan out?" He simply gives without reserve, constantly pouring out of Himself. Understanding this, we can thank

Him for His awesome loving kindness and follow His example. When we conform to His character, we reflect His likeness to the dying, lost world. They will notice by our generous attitude that there is something special about us.

Economic Principle:
giving and taking the right way.

That night God appeared to Solomon and said to him, "Ask for whatever you want me to give you." Solomon answered God, "You have shown great kindness to David my father and have made me king in his place. Now, LORD God, let your promise to my father David be confirmed, you have made me king over a people who are as numerous as the dust of the earth. Give me wisdom and knowledge, that I may lead this people, for who is able to govern this great people of yours?' God said to Solomon, "Since this is your heart's desire and you have not asked for wealth, riches or honor, not for the death of your enemies, and since you have not asked for a long life but for wisdom and knowledge to govern my people over whom I have made you king, therefore wisdom and knowledge will be given you. And I will also give you wealth, riches and honor, such as no king who was before you ever had and none after you will have." 2 Chronicles 1:7-12

What important lesson can we take away from this passage? Simply put, God knows the motives of our hearts. Even if we fool ourselves into believing we have good intent, the Lord can see right past the facade. Proverbs 16:2 says "A man's ways seem innocent to him, but motives are weighed by the LORD."

Asking for the right things demonstrates our maturity in Christ. Solomon did not ask for anything he could see or touch, or for vengeance on his enemies, but he did petition for wisdom and knowledge. This shows that his mind was not on earthly things, but spiritual things. It also displays the value godly qualities held in his life. Ineffable qualities such as wisdom and knowledge are not carelessly given, nor are they for sale. The Lord is their keeper and He distributes them as He sees fit. God knew Solomon's heart was void of selfish ambition so He gave him what he asked.

We apply this to our lives by constantly checking and rechecking why we do what we do. How do we handle money? What do we buy? Are we using people to get what we want? We must talk to God, seek Him, and allow the Holy Spirit to correct us if we are wrong. Asking for godly attributes will improve the people we are on the inside, instead of dolling up the outside. James 1:5 says that "If any of [us] lacks wisdom, [we] should ask God, who gives generously to all without finding fault, and it will be given to [us]."

Prayer of Change

Father God, I realize that the intentions of my heart are not always righteous. I ask your forgiveness. Lord, I want to give lots of things, more than just my money. I also want to learn to give with a cheerful heart. Help me to refrain from giving belligerently or with the hopes of receiving something in return. I pray this in Jesus' name. Amen.

Tithing

Economic Principle:
giving a tenth of your income.

"Will a man rob God? Yet you rob me. But you ask, 'How do we rob you?' In tithes and offerings. You are under a curse—the whole nation of you—because you are robbing me. Bring the whole tithe into the storehouse, that there may be food in my house. Test me in this," says the LORD *Almighty, "and see if I will not throw open the floodgates of heaven and pour out so much blessing that you will not have room enough for it. I will prevent pests from devouring your crops, and the vines in your fields will not cast their fruit," says the* LORD *Almighty. "Then all the nations will call you blessed, for yours will be a delightful land," says the* LORD *Almighty."* Malachi 3:8-12

Just think how great he was: Even the patriarch Abraham gave him a tenth of the plunder! Hebrews 7:4

"Blessed be God Most High, who has delivered your enemies into your hand." And he gave him a tenth of all. Genesis 14:20

Moreover, you shall speak to the Levites and say to them, "When you take from the sons of Israel the tithe which I have given you from them for your inheritance, then you shall present an offering from it to the LORD, *a tithe of the tithe."* Numbers 18:26

*Woe to you, teachers of the law and Pharisees, you hyp-
ocrites! You give a tenth of your spices—mint, dill and
cummin. But you have neglected the more important
matters of the law—justice, mercy and faithfulness. You
should have practiced the latter, without neglecting the
former.* Matthew 23:23

*Enter Bethel and transgress; in Gilgal multiply trans-
gression! Bring your sacrifices every morning, your
tithes every three days. "Offer a thank offering also from
that which is leavened, and proclaim freewill offerings,
make them known. For so you love to do, you sons of
Israel," declares the Lord God.* Amos 4:4-5

*Concerning the collection for the saints, as I directed the
churches of Galatia, so do you also. On the first day of
every week let each one of you put aside and save, as he
may prosper, so that no collections be made when I
come.* 1 Corinthians 16:1-2

*All those about them encouraged them with articles of sil-
ver, with gold, with goods, with cattle and with valuables,
aside from all that was given as a freewill offering.* Ezra 1:6

*The first of all the first fruits of every kind and every
contribution of every kind, from all your contributions,
shall be for the priests; you shall also give to the priest
the first of your dough to cause a blessing to rest on your
house.* Ezekiel 44:30

What about tithing? Does this issue apply to us today?
Well, if you read any of the verses we quoted earlier,
you would know that tithing is mandatory in a Christian's life.

The word "tithe" literally means one tenth. This is the minimum amount a believer should give. The Jews gave much more than ten percent but God commanded a mandatory ten percent tithe. He did this to teach us the heart issue underneath the economic one: We can never outgive God. He gave His only Son to die on the cross in our place, the place our sin earned us. But Jesus cancelled the debt and besides saving us from hell, He lavished on us eternal life in His presence forever. How could any human possibly come close to repaying that, or even become worthy of receiving it for that matter? Surely none of us could, hence the reason we simply accept His free gift. The joy of being saved from eternal damnation should make our hearts overflow with generosity, the same characteristic every genuine believer has experienced at Calvary.

The concept of tithing should not threaten us but encourage us. We will not lose our salvation because we have only been giving three percent of our income, but we should take this admonition as an opportunity to improve our giving process. Some people like to make a personal "deal" with God, promising to read their Bible more or go to church twice a week in exchange for keeping more money for themselves. They trade what they are not willing to do with what they *do* want to do. Who are we to bargain with God? These kinds of people have *completely* missed the point. They are making serving God into a chore, which will eventually make them resentful, failing to see that the Lord can use them as a tool to bless others and help spread the gospel. They forfeit God's blessing because they choose to run their lives their own way, completely forgetting that the Lord is owner of all and capable of inflicting punishment. They sacrifice the chance to grow through God's refining process and subject themselves to a life of mediocrity and complacency.

However, those who choose to live above this realize they have been given control of certain assets and want to share them to benefit others. They understand that God is not into playing tug-of-war and would much rather bless than have to administer a lesson the hard way. They see giving as fun, a method of delighting themselves and others. Someday in heaven, we will see all the opportunities we had and the eternal consequences of either lavishing or hoarding a gift.

If you are thinking that tithe starts after paying off debt, think again, my friend. The Bible never says to tithe *after* you have paid your debts. In fact, it says the exact opposite. When your paycheck comes, pay the tithe *first* and then your other bills. The Lord will bless you for your faithfulness.

Tithing is not to be done once a year, or whenever we feel like writing a check. First Corinthians 16:2 says to set aside our money at the beginning of the week. A good rule of thumb is to tithe the following Sunday after receiving your paycheck. This way, we never lose track of when or how much to give. The Lord has determined this process to be the best because He knows that His house is the storehouse for all believers. Churches must have a regular cash flow in order to pay bills and administer to the needs of the congregation. If we paid our tithe at the end of the year in one lump sum, it would not help when a crisis hits the church in May. As employees, we do not receive a paycheck once a year. Expenses are ongoing and a budget is hard to plan because unexpected things are happening all the time. Similarly, the church must have a regular flow of funds to maintain its purpose to spread the gospel and minister to the needs of believers.

Tithing, and all money-related issues for that matter, can cause division in a marriage. Spouses are not always going to agree on the amount or location to give. Even the *kinds* of gifts can cause strife among mates. But the best way to counter these problems is to remember 1 Corinthians 13:3: "If I give all I possess to the poor and surrender my body to the flames, but have not love, I am nothing." Satan wants us to get in arguments over giving because it usually leads to *not* giving, damaging our relationships, or both. Blaming each other or refusing to compromise only causes resentment and finger pointing.

If you and your spouse disagree over tithing, sit down and consider what the Bible has to say about giving and the amount of money or things each of you is willing to give. Next, consider how each of you would like to administer that gift. If you can both come to the same conclusions from Scripture, then you have already won half the battle! Take time to listen to each other's concerns, however, because prizing relationships are at the top of God's list when it comes to living in His economy.

Prayer of Change

Heavenly Father, I see that tithing is not just a way for churches to ask for money but that you actually command it in your Word. I admit that sometimes I do not give ten percent and I pretend like I forgot to do it. Lord, I never want to cheat you because you have never cheated me. I realize that this is my opportunity to give back to you out of the thankfulness of my heart. Lord, teach me important habits in my tithing so I don't miss out on the blessing you have for me. Help me to apply these lessons to my life. I pray this in Jesus' name. Amen.

Giving to the Church

Economic Principle:
giving and responding to the call.

King David rose to his feet and said: "Listen to me, my brothers and my people. I had it in my heart to build a house as a place of rest for the ark of the covenant of the LORD, for the footstool of our God, and I made plans to build it." 1 Chronicles 28:2

He said to me: "Solomon your son is the one who will build my house and my courts, for I have chosen him to be my son, and I will be his father." 1 Chronicles 28:6

And you, my son Solomon, acknowledge the God of your father, and serve him with wholehearted devotion and with a willing mind, for the LORD searches every heart and understands every motive behind the thoughts. If you seek him, he will be found by you; but if you forsake him, he will reject you forever. 1 Chronicles 28:9

With all my resources I have provided for the temple of my God. 1 Chronicles 29:2a

Besides, in my devotion to the temple of my God, I now give my personal treasures of gold and silver for the temple of my God, over and above everything I have provided for this holy temple. 1 Chronicles 29:3

"Now, who is willing to consecrate himself today to the LORD?" Then the leaders of the families, the officers of

the tribes of Israel, the commanders of thousands and commanders of hundreds, and the officials in charge of the king's work gave willingly. 1 Chronicles 29:5b-6

The people rejoiced at the willing response of the leaders, for they had given freely and wholeheartedly to the LORD. 1 Chronicles 29:9

But who am I, and who are my people, that we should be able to give generously as this? Everything has come from you, and we have given you only what comes from your hand. 1 Chronicles 29:14

O LORD *our God, as for all this abundance that we have provided for building you a temple for your Holy Name, it comes from your hand, and all of it belongs to you. I know, my God, that you test the heart and are pleased with integrity. All these things I have given willingly and with honest intent. And now I have seen with joy how willingly your people who are here have given to you.* 1 Chronicles 29:16-17

The economic principle to learn here is that of giving and responding to the call. In recent years, some church leaders have brought professional fundraisers to "teach" the membership how to raise and manage donations. This is unnecessary and even unscriptural because God's Word already gives us a system to raise funds.

The leadership's role is to listen to God, understand the needs of the congregation, pray about and envision the future plans and missions of the church, and give to the campaign with honest, willing hearts. Once they accomplish these points, they must communicate them to the people. Managing and charting the progress towards these goals is also essential; this way everyone is aware the church is changing.

The purpose of expanding ministries is to give back to God. Leaders should not push their personal dreams down the throats of the congregation or convey a sense of "do or die," because the church's existence is for furthering the gospel, not keeping up with the Joneses.

We, as members, should take what is presented to us and pray about it. We should submit to our church leaders, but always to the Lord first. If we do decide to give, it must be done cheerfully and faithfully, without grudge or feeling of obligation.

Whatever David gave to the Lord (which was quite a bit), he acknowledged that it had initially been received from Him. He also challenged the nation to give sacrificially. With a godly example to follow, Israel consecrated themselves through their love gifts. These were not pledges or promises to give later on; these were concrete gifts actually given. There were no whiners, complainers, or beggars—just givers with happy hearts.

This passage serves as a great example of how to campaign for the Lord's work. But suppose that we disagree with the projects presented in the church body. First, we must test our heart in prayer to see if we are harboring any bitterness towards a particular plan or leader. We must be sure we have not been caught up in a competitive way of thinking. Second, we must present our ideas and concerns to the elders in a loving and humble matter. These ideas must be void of any selfish ambition. If we have questions, we should ask them! There is absolutely nothing wrong with getting clarification. The Lord blesses good intentions.

Prayer of Change

Lord, these scriptures in the book of Chronicles are important lessons. Help me to learn and listen carefully to your economic principle. Help me to give and respond to you and my church leaders in faithfulness, not in stubbornness.

All I have is yours, Lord. You have given me all I have for your glory and honor. I stand ready to give of my property, my talents, and my very being for your purposes, especially if that includes expanding a current ministry. I pray that my church leadership would seek your face, hear your Word, and obey it. Help them and me to be humble in doing your will. In Jesus' name I pray. Amen.

CAUSE AND EFFECT

Economic Principle:
reaping what you sow.

Honor the LORD with your wealth, with the firstfruits of all your crops; then your barns will be filled to overflowing, and your vats will brim over with new wine.
Proverbs 3:9-10

Give, and it will be given to you. A good measure, pressed down, shaken together and running over, will be poured into your lap. For with the measure you use, it will be measured to you. Luke 6:38

Remember this: Whoever sows sparingly will also reap sparingly, and whoever sows generously will also reap generously. Each man should give what he has decided in his heart to give, not reluctantly or under compulsion, for God loves a cheerful giver. And God is able to make all grace abound to you, so that in all things at all times, having all that you need, you will abound in every good work. As it is written: "He has scattered abroad his gifts to the poor, his righteousness endures forever." Now he who supplies seed to the sower and bread for food will also supply and increase your store of seed and will enlarge the harvest of your righteousness. You will be made rich in every way so that you can be generous on every occasion, and through us your generosity will result in thanksgiving to God. This service that you perform is not only supplying the needs of

God's people but is also overflowing in many expressions of thanks to God. Because of the service by which you have proved yourselves, men will praise God for the obedience that accompanies your confession of the gospel of Christ, and for your generosity in sharing with them and with everyone else. 2 Corinthians 9:6-13

There is one who scatters, yet increases all the more, and there is one who withholds what is justly due, and ye it results only in want. The generous man will be prosperous, and he who waters will himself be watered. Proverbs 11:24-25

Another one of God's principles is the cause-and-effect principle. This means, if we do something, God will do something in return. If we give with cheerful hearts, God promises to bless us. In Malachi He said He would open the floodgates and pour out so much blessing we would not have room for it! That seems hard to believe, but since God said it, it must be true. We can hold firm to His Word, but we have to keep up our end of the deal as well. The generous giver does not worry about God's part because he trusts in the provision for his needs. The cheerful giver does not fall prey to "prosperity teaching."

The real intent of prosperity teaching is to gain. People enthralled with this idea ask, "Why wouldn't God want me to be rich?" That would be an easily answered question if they had a Bible in their hands! Being wealthy causes a person to love what they have more than the God they serve. Material possessioins quickly become an idol and trust shifts off the Sustainer and onto the things. Materialism is a horrible danger because not only does it open up doors for greed, envy, and pride, but it also blinds a person from seeing what a *real* need is. Unfortunately, in America we think we *need* a Starbucks in order to make it through the day, or that we *need* a two-story house on beach-front property. A true need involves food, clothing, shelter, and anything else necessary for survival. We do not need coffee; we *need* water. We do not need a two-story house; we *need* a roof over our heads. Materialism has completely tainted our ability to label a genuine need; that is why God does not want some people to be rich. He knows what best suits us and what is absolutely necessary for our life and spiritual walk.

The cause-and-effect method can be likened to sowing and reaping. Paul said that if we sow sparingly, we will reap sparingly and likewise with sowing bountifully. A Christian's sowing job was clearly stated in the Great Commission. We are to spread the gospel as abundantly as if a farmer were planting seeds. Some of the seeds will grow to produce a great harvest, just like the life of one born-again believer will affect many others. We are to shower others as if we were a fresh water hose, because if we bless others, we ourselves will be blessed. Proverbs 11:25 exclaims that if we water others we ourselves will be watered. When we *cause* a blessing in another's life, the effects are twofold: that person will thank God, and that person will praise God. We, being willing vessels of the Lord's work, complete the cycle of bringing the Father glory. We are the hoses that spray out God's good gifts to others so they can grow up healthy and strong, waving praises back to heaven. What a beautiful cycle we have the opportunity to be a part of!

Prayer of Change

Almighty God, I don't want my view of how I should live on this earth to be tainted by prosperity teaching. Sometimes I get so sucked in that I can't tell what a real need is. Lord, teach me discernment in this area so I am not spending beyond my limits. Father, I want to give abundantly so that I can reap abundantly because you promised it! I believe what you promised and want to take you up on the offer, but I will need your grace and mercy because I am constantly falling back into my sinful ways. Thank you, Jesus, for providing me such special rewards! In Jesus' name I pray. Amen.

SACRIFICIAL GIVING

Economic Principle:
what is an acceptable gift?

In the course of time Cain brought some of the fruits of the soil as an offering to the LORD. But Abel brought fat portions from some of the firstborn of his flock. The LORD looked with favor on Abel and his offering, but on Cain and his offering he did not look with favor. So Cain was very angry, and his face was downcast. Then the LORD said to Cain, "Why are you angry? Why is your face downcast? If you do what is right, will you not be accepted? But if you do not do what is right, sin is crouching at your door; it desires to have you, but you must master it." Genesis 4:3-7

What economic principle is God teaching here? Clearly, we know that Abel's gift was acceptable, while Cain's was not. God knew that the heart of the two brothers was not the same. Abel's offering was made with a cheerful and joyful heart, Cain's was not. In fact, if we read on in the text we see that Cain argued with God with a belligerent attitude. He had an unyielding and un-submissive disposition towards the Lord. His bad attitude came from the obligation he felt to offer a sacrifice to God. Cain wanted to fool the Lord, trying to slide by without being noticed. God was not pleased, to say the least.

God did not need Cain or Abel's offering. Nor does He need ours. He already owns everything! He is more concerned with the motive for our offering and the attitude with which it is given. Abel's motive was pure and Cain realized that. Because

Abel's offering was acceptable, Cain became jealous to the point of murder.

In verse 4 it says that Abel brought fat portions of the first-born of his flock. He did not give the animals with limps or diseases, but the best of what he had. Abel walked with the Lord in a reverent way. Cain, however, was disrespectful. He lied and said he did not know where Abel was when the Lord asked him. Did Cain really think that the Creator of the universe did not know where Abel was? God was giving him an opportunity to come clean and repent. Instead, Cain denied the Lord's omniscience and went down in history as the first murderer.

The principle of God's economy in this passage is to give with a joyful, cheerful, and obedient heart. Our heart must be contrite, giving because of thankfulness and not out of compulsion. Second Corinthians 9:7 says the Lord loves a cheerful giver.

Let these scriptures change the way we apply this lesson to our lives by engaging in an upright relationship with the Lord. We should seek Him with a heart that wants to give of our self, not withhold. Trusting God with our life and provisions will give us an attitude of gratefulness. This will lead to more laughing, smiling, and reduced depression! Let's give with good intent when we give to our local church or ministry, not with a "What will I get out of this?" mentality. This includes giving things like time, talents, blood, belongings, and anything else that can be used to bless God's family and bring Him glory. Giving is not just something we do, it is someone we are.

As you live, be creative and look for opportunities to give. Perhaps ministering to residents of a nursing home is something you would like to do. Bring your children along and show them the right attitude for giving. They learn from our examples.

Prayer of Change

Jesus, help me to look for more opportunities to give of myself and my possessions. When I give to others, remind me that I am really giving to you. I trust you to provide for me when I give beyond my means. I pray this in Jesus' name. Amen.

Economic Principle:
how to be an example of sacrificial giving.

And now brothers, we want you to know about the grace that God has given the Macedonian churches. Out of the most severe trial, their overflowing joy and extreme poverty welled up in rich generosity. For I testify that they gave as much as they were able, and beyond their ability. Entirely on their own, they urgently pleaded with us for the privilege of sharing in the service to the saints. 2 Corinthians 8:1-4

These people deserve to be in the Hall of Fame for giving! We can definitely see why Paul wrote about them, because they were great examples of *sacrificial* giving.

These people lived in a region where war had crippled their economy and left them in poverty. The Romans had plundered them and they were persecuted nearly every day, but they never let this hardship hinder their confidence in God. They let God's grace transform their attitudes into ones zealous to give.

The Macedonians were committed to God, willing to yield their needs to meet the needs of others. Webster's dictionary defines sacrifice as "to suffer loss; or something given up or lost for the sake of something else. To offer to deity something precious." Sacrificial giving is the ultimate giving if motivated and grounded in love for God through Jesus Christ. The Macedonians suffered, but they gave despite facing affliction. This scripture passage illustrates precisely why anyone who argues that he does not have to give in such a situation is completely ungrounded in his thinking and wrong in his attitude. The Macedonians did not keep their eyes on their horrendous circumstances, but on the Lord and His commands. They gave beyond their ability, trusting that God would compensate them later. No one forced them to give. They viewed it as a privilege to help fellow believers. We would do well to imitate their example and apply these lessons to our lives.

Prayer of Change

Father God, I want to be an example of sacrificial giving like the Macedonian church. I know that through your Word and Spirit I can be spurred on to do that. When the opportunity comes, help me to welcome it and not shun it. In Jesus' name I pray. Amen.

Economic Principle:
surrendering all in a time of need.

Jesus sat down opposite the place where the offerings were put and watched the crowd putting their money into the temple treasury. Many rich threw in large amounts. But a poor widow came and put two very small copper coins, worth only a fraction of a penny. Calling his disciples to him, Jesus said, "I tell you the truth, this poor widow has put more into the treasury than all the others. They all gave out of their wealth; but she, out of her poverty, put in everything—she had to live on." Mark 12:41-44

As he looked up, Jesus saw the rich putting their gifts into the temple treasury. He also saw a poor widow put in two very small copper coins. "I tell you the truth," he said, "this poor widow has put in more than all the others. All these people gave their gifts out of their wealth; but she out of her poverty put in all she had to live on." Luke 21:1-4

These scriptures perfectly portray God's economy because this story is based on such principles as sacrificial giving. For this story to be mentioned twice in Scripture means it is extra important. The widow's giving was so impressive that Jesus stopped everything and commanded His disciples to watch. Now there is a giver for the Hall of Fame!

What we as humans find fascinating or how we think things should work is not always the case in God's economy. God's ways are higher than our ways. How could two small coins in any regular world economy add up to more than the rest of the money in the treasury? That does not make any sense! But Jesus completely tore down that way of thinking and showed us the real value behind the widow's gift. She gave "all she had to live on." Now if that is not a sacrificial gift, what would be?

While the Pharisees and scribes were being piously arrogant in their motivations, this widow was motivated by love and purpose. She surrendered everything she had for the work of the Lord. In earthly terms it was the smallest possible gift, but in God's economy it was the greatest. Her gift amounted to more because it was a sacrificial gift based on trust for God to provide, while the rich gave only small portions of the large sums they still had in reserves. Here we can see once again that, the Lord is concerned with the heart issue underneath the one *we* may think is important.

In God's economy even the tiniest gift is significant. Who we are and what we have *is* important to the Lord if we are willing to be molded by His infinite wisdom. Because sacrificial giving is not based on numerical value, giving a penny with a servant's heart is invaluable!

Does this mean that even if we are giving small amounts, it will not be difficult? Of course not! If anything, giving small amounts in the midst of financial adversity makes one keenly aware of his tight position. But it also gives the Lord a bigger window of opportunity to surprise and bless the recipient. When those numbers get low in our checkbook, fear and insecurity may set in, especially if we write another check for tithe. But exercising our ability to give on a regular basis, even *beyond* our ability, builds up our spiritual muscles for giving. We cannot expect to walk into the gym for the first time and bench press 225 pounds. Neither can we expect to enjoy sacrificial giving if we are not practicing it regularly.

Prayer of Change

Mighty Lord, this section really gives me some food for thought because of all the great examples mentioned. I want to be one of them! Jesus, I understand that giving with the same attitude as the widow did will be hard for me because I have so much more than she did, but I know that with your guidance I can move closer and closer to having that attitude. Begin this work in me even as I pray this right now. In Jesus' name I pray. Amen.

GIVING TO CHARITY

Economic Principle:
giving to neighbors and strangers alike.

Jesus said, "A man was going down from Jerusalem to Jericho, when he fell into the hands of robbers. They stripped him of his clothes, beat him and went away, leaving him half dead. A priest happened to be going down the same road, and when he saw the man, he passed by on the other side. So too, a Levite, when he came to the place and saw him, passed by on the other side. But a Samaritan, as he traveled, came where the man was; and when he saw him, he took pity on him. He went to him and bandaged his wounds, pouring on oil and wine. Then he put the man on his own donkey, took him to an inn and took care of him. The next day he took out two silver coins and gave them to the innkeeper. 'Look after him,' he said, 'and when I return I will reimburse you for any extra expense you may have.' Which one of these do you think was a neighbor to the man who fell into the hands of robbers?" The expert in the law replied, "The one who had mercy on him." Jesus told him, "Go and do likewise." Luke 10:30-37

What good is it, my brothers, if a man claims to have faith but has no deeds? Can such faith save him? Suppose a brother or sister is without clothes and daily food. If one of you says to him, "Go, I wish you well; keep warm and well fed," but does nothing about his physical needs, what good is it? In the same way, faith

by itself, if it is not accompanied by action, is dead.
James 2:14-17

When you reap the harvest of your land, moreover, you shall not reap to the very corners of your field nor gather the gleaning of the harvest; you are to leave for the needy and the alien. I am the LORD *your God.*
Leviticus 23:22

I delivered the poor who cried for help, and the orphan who had no helper. Job 29:12

You shall not oppress a hired servant who is poor and needy, whether he is one of your countrymen or one of your aliens who is in your land in your towns. You shall give him his wages on his day before the sun sets, for he is poor and sets his heart on it; so that he may not cry against you to the LORD *and it become sin in you.*
Deuteronomy 24:14-15

He has given freely to the poor; His righteousness endures forever; His horn will be exalted in honor. Psalm 112:9

I know that the LORD *will maintain the cause of the afflicted and justice for the poor.* Psalm 140:12

He who oppresses the poor taunts his Maker, but he who is gracious to the needy honors Him. Proverbs 14:31

He who gives to the poor will never want, but he who shuts his eyes will have many curses. Proverbs 28:27

The righteous is concerned for the rights of the poor, the wicked does not understand such concern. Proverbs 29:7

Open your mouth, judge righteously, and defend the rights of the afflicted and needy. Proverbs 31:9

Jesus said to him, "If you wish to be complete, go and sell your possessions and give to the poor, and you will have treasure in heaven; and come, follow Me." Matthew 19:21

He would answer and say to them, "The man who has two tunics is to share with him who has none; and he who has good is to do likewise." Luke 3:11

Sell your possessions and give to charity; make yourselves money belts which do not wear out, an unfailing treasure in heaven, where no thief comes near nor moth destroys. Luke 12:33

All those who had believed were together and had all things in common; and they began selling their property and possessions and were sharing them with all, as anyone might have need. Acts 2:44-45

Jesus used the parable of the Good Samaritan to teach His listeners how to have a humble and merciful heart. Two people who should have been the first to exercise compassion, the priest and the Levite, were the ones who turned their heads and voluntarily denied the injured man the help he needed. They justified their actions on the basis of being busy and not wanting to become unclean. What they failed to understand was precisely what Jesus was trying to teach: We must love our neighbors sacrificially.

Neighbors are not just the people who live next door to us; they are strangers, people we have never met. The Samaritan recognized that this beat-up man was his neighbor, despite his ethnicity, social status, and financial position. He chose to give sacrificially by taking responsibility for the man's care. He used his time, strength, and money to provide for his needs. He was no doubt a busy man, or else he would not have been traveling on the road, but his business duties did not hinder his duty to love his neighbor. Jesus wants us to give of ourselves as the Samaritan did. He exhorts us to sacrifice not only financially, but in all the areas in which we have something to give.

As our journey continues in knowing, understanding, and applying God's economic principles in our everyday life, we must recognize and forget the things we learned growing up that are opposed to the Lord's teachings. From early on, we may have observed examples of stinginess, cheapness, and withholding. If this is true, then let's look at a recipe for dealing with these problems.

Check all the statements that apply to you and your childhood:

- Being stingy was considered a positive attribute
- Being cheap was a way of getting an edge over others
- Giving money was avoided at all costs
- I was taught giving to get
- My parents argued about where and what to give
- Donating happened only when we did not need something any longer
- I witnessed a parent rummaging through someone else's trash

- There was no concept of sacrificial giving
- In a local community crisis, we stayed uninvolved
- Favoritism was shown to siblings
- Parents looked for recognition from giving for personal esteem

By now you have probably noticed that in order to change, we must know what we are changing from. Understanding the past helps give us direction for our future. We also want to continue in a positive direction for the sake of bringing God glory and deepening our walk as believers. Taking this "quiz" shows us how we handle our money today, and if we match what we *do* against what God says we *should* do, we can see where we are off track.

Next, we simply replace our current habits by practicing godly ones. Ephesians 4:22-24 can encourage us and give us a mental picture of dressing ourselves in those acts of righteousness we need to exhibit: "You were taught, with regard to your former way of life, to put off your old self, which is being corrupted by its deceitful desires; to be made new in the attitude of your minds; and to put on the new self, created to be like God in true righteousness and holiness." The Lord wants us to work on trusting Him more while we move towards Him on our spiritual journey.

Knowing the economy of God must be step number one. Applying the truth we learn is number two. Step number three is receiving all the rewards we are promised for obedience and a servant's heart, even if we have to wait until heaven to receive them. In the grasp of eternity, it really is not that long.

So let's sum up what the scriptures have taught us. Through the Holy Word, the Spirit will guide and convict us in the areas we need to grow. Then we will pray and ask the Lord to enable us during our struggles so we may be counted faithful servants.

Lessons about Giving

- I will give in secret and not for show (Matthew 6:1-4)
- I will sow generously and cheerfully (2 Corinthians 9:6-13)
- I will tithe, recognizing that God has ownership (Matthew 23:23)
- I will tithe off of my gross income, not net (Proverbs 3:9-10)
- I will be a "garden hose" of giving (Proverbs 11:24-25)
- I will give to help the needy (Acts 4:32-37)
- I recognize all I have was given to me by God (1 Chronicles 29:14)
- I will give honestly (1 Chronicles 29:17)
- I will go out of my way to give and help others (Luke 10:30-37)
- I will give to the poor (Leviticus 23:22)
- I will not turn my head when others need help (Proverbs 28:27)
- I will desire treasures in heaven (Luke 12:33)
- I will give regularly and consistently (1 Corinthians 16:1-2)
- I will give sacrificially (Mark 12:41-44)
- I will focus on giving, not receiving (Acts 20:35)
- I will give with a loving heart (1 Corinthians 13:3)
- I will thank God for what He has given me (John 3:16)
- I will give to strangers, prisoners, and the sick (Matthew 25:35-45)

Prayer of Change

Almighty God, no one can outgive you. You are the greatest giver of all time! Your love, mercy, and forgiveness overflow through your Son Jesus Christ and bless my life. Thank you for giving me all I own, my abilities, and time to develop relationships. I want to learn to give like you do, Lord. Help me escape the fear that may set in when I step out in faith. Give me eyes to recognize opportunities I might have to bless others. Fill my heart with sensitivity and compassion so that I can bestow grace on others like you did for me on the cross. Father, I trust that you will provide for me when I give sacrificially.

Thank you for the opportunity to learn how I can transform my life in the area of giving. May your Word dwell in my heart and mind so that I never forget these lessons. I pray this in Jesus' name. Amen.

Part 3

STEWARDSHIP

What We Can Handle

Economic Principle:
God never gives too much or too little.

Again, it will be like a man going on a journey, who called his servants and entrusted his property to them. To one he gave five talents of money, to another two talents, and to another one talent, each according to his ability. Then he went on his journey. The man who had received the five talents went at once and put his money to work and gained five more. So also, the one with the two talents gained two more. But the man who had received the one talent went off, dug a hole in the ground and hid his master's money.

After a long time the master of those servants returned and settled accounts with them. The man who had received the five talents brought the other five. "Master," he said, "you entrusted me with five talents. See, I have gained five more." His master replied, "Well done, good and faithful servant! You have been faithful with a few things; I will put you in charge of many things. Come and share your master's happiness!"

The man with the two talents also came. "Master," he said, "you entrusted me with two talents; see, I have gained two more." His master replied, "Well done, good and faithful servant! You have been faithful with a few things; I will put you in charge of many things. Come and share in your master's happiness!"

Then the man with the one talent came. "Master," he said, "I knew that you are a hard man, harvesting where you have not sown and gathering where you have not gathered seed. So I was afraid and went out and hid your talent in the ground. See, here is what belongs to you." His master replied, "You wicked and lazy servant! So you knew that I harvest where I have not sown and gather where I have not gathered seed? Well then, you should have put my money on deposit with the bankers, so that when I returned I would have received it back with interest. Take the talent from him and give it to the one who has ten talents. For everyone who has will be given more, and he will have an abundance. Whoever does not have, even what he has will be taken from him. And throw that worthless servant outside, into the darkness, where there will be weeping and gnashing of teeth." Matthew 25:14-30

Stewardship is defined as managing another's property and resources. Since we learned earlier that God is the Creator and Owner of all things, it is His materials we are entrusted with. Our role is to play the part of manager for the Lord's divine purposes. We bring Him glory when we obey so that the entire world can witness His majesty. In a biblical setting, a steward is also someone who will be repaid for his actions. There will be a day of reckoning for his decisions, judgments, and choices. The faithful will receive their reward while the unfaithful will receive only discipline.

Webster defines stewardship as "an individual's responsibility to manage his life and property with proper regard for the rights of others." So even in a secular view, we see that as believers, we have a moral obligation to manage our affairs in an exemplary fashion. This highlights our obedience and glorifies God.

The first lesson on stewardship is taken from the parable of the talents. Jesus starts out by stating that the employer is going away. He does not say to where or for how long he is going, but he does leave three servants with three different amounts of talents to manage. He gave to each steward "according to his own ability." This is the key phrase in helping Christians understand one of God's major economic principles. The Lord entrusts us with no more or no less than we can handle. If He gave us too much, we could become overwhelmed with the burden or become disinclined to make any efforts at all. If we gave a five-year-old the responsibility of mowing the lawn, not only would he be unable to complete the task, but he would also learn to hate being asked to do any other chores. The Lord uses the same principle with believers.

In the same way that God does not give us more than we can handle, He makes sure we are reaching our potential. Not giving us enough challenging situations would cause us to become lazy and trust more in our own abilities instead of on the Lord. If we asked a seventeen-year-old to take out the trash, he could complete the task in a matter of minutes. He has the capability to take out the trash, clean his room, wash the dishes, *and* mow the lawn! His potential is greater because he has learned responsibility. But if we let him get away with only one chore, he would most likely become a couch potato, unwilling to help with any other family chores. So we see that the Lord giving each believer the amount of responsibility he can handle keeps the believer's life in balance while growing closer to godly perfection.

Who is to say what ability each servant has? God, of course. He knows us better than we know ourselves. He also sees what we can become or what we can digress to. He understands how much responsibility will keep us running at top-notch speed.

Prayer of Change

Jesus, I believe that you will not give me more than what I can handle. I also believe that you will give me enough working potential to reach my ultimate output. You have given me many abilities. Show me how I can use those for your glory. I look forward to being perfect with you in heaven one day, Savior, but until then, I ask for your help and guidance as I walk through everyday life. I pray this in Jesus' name. Amen.

WORK AND LAZINESS

Economic Principle:
the good steward works diligently.

*Whatever you do, do your work heartily, as for the Lord
rather than for men.* Colossians 3:23

The precious possession of a man is diligence.
Proverbs 12:27

*Whatever your hand finds to do, do it with all your
might.* Ecclesiastes 9:10

*Encourage the young women to love their husbands, to
love their children, to be sensible, pure, workers at
home.* Titus 2:4-5

*A wife of noble character who can find? She is worth
far more than rubies. Her husband has full confidence
in her and lacks nothing of value. She brings him
good, not harm, all the days of her life. She selects
wool and flax and works with eager hands. She is like
the merchant ships, bringing her food from afar. She
gets up while it is still dark; she provides food for her
family and portions for her servant girls. She consid-
ers a field and buys it; out of her earnings she plants a
vineyard. She sets about her work vigorously; her
arms are strong for her tasks. She sees that her trading
is profitable, and her lamp does not go out at night. In
her hand she holds the distaff and grasps the spindle*

with her fingers. She opens her arms to the poor and extends her hand to the needy. When it snows, she has no fear for her household, for all of them are clothed in scarlet. She makes coverings for her bed; she is clothed in fine linen and purple. Her husband is respected at the city gate, when he takes his seat among the elders of the land. She makes linen garments and sells them, and supplies the merchants with sashes. She is clothed in strength and dignity; she can laugh at the days to come. She speaks with wisdom, and faithful instruction is on her tongue. She watches over her affairs of her household and does not eat the bread of idleness. Her children arise and call her blessed; her husband also and he praises her, "Many women do noble things, but you surpass them all." Charm is deceptive, and beauty is fleeting, but a woman who fears the LORD *is to be praised. Give her the reward she has earned, and let her works bring her praise at the city gates.* Proverbs 31:10-31

Even when we were with you, we used to give you this rule: If a man will not work, he shall not eat.
2 Thessalonians 3:10

A worker's appetite works for him, for his hunger urges him on. Proverbs 16:26

The hard-working farmer ought to be the first to receive his share of the crops. 2 Timothy 2:6

Every man who eats and drinks sees good in all his labor—it is the gift of God. Ecclesiastes 3:13

He who works his land will have abundant food, but the one who chases fantasies will have his fill of poverty. Proverbs 28:19

Poor is he who works with a negligent hand, but the hand of the diligent makes rich. Proverbs 10:4

A lazy man does not roast his prey, but the precious possession of a man is diligence. Proverbs 12:27

The soul of the sluggard craves and gets nothing, but the soul of the diligent is made fat. Proverbs 13:4

He also who is slack in his work is brother to him who destroys. Proverbs 18:9

Laziness casts into a deep sleep, and an idle man will suffer hunger. Proverbs 19:15

If anyone does not provide for his relatives, and especially for his immediate family, he has denied the faith and is worse than an unbeliever. 1 Timothy 5:8

The heavy drinker and the glutton will come to poverty. Proverbs 23:21

Drawing from the before-mentioned parable of the talents, the owner went on his journey, and verse 16 says the faithful servants "immediately" went to work. That implies eagerness and ambition. The servant who received the five talents doubled his master's money, as did the servant who received the two talents. The third servant, however, hid his talent in the ground, perhaps out of laziness or hoping his boss would forget the matter.

When the owner returned and the day of accounting drew nigh, the owner did not forget what he had entrusted his servants with. In fact, he was eagerly expecting the results. The two faithful servants presented their doubled profits and they were commended with the words, "Well done, good and faithful servant!" They were able to partake in their master's happiness, as we believers will be able to partake in God's happiness if we are faithful.

The third servant was not so jubilantly commended. The master called him a "wicked and lazy slave" because he had not even thought to put the money in the bank to gain interest! His talent was taken away and given to the servant with the ten talents, and he was thrown into the darkness, where there is "weeping and gnashing of teeth." The unbeliever who tries to "skate" by—doing as little as possible while still hoping to receive the blessings—will be brought to recompense and will receive the consequence he has brought upon himself.

This passage can be viewed as a staircase lesson. When we can learn to step carefully and effectively on each succeeding step, we can climb higher and higher. God will give us more to do and it will be exciting to engage in His plan. Our life has meaning *because* we are a part of God's economy. It allows us to feel joy and satisfaction. Obedience gives us purpose—the mission to glorify God, minister to those around us, and show God we love Him.

In John 14:21 Jesus says, "Whoever has my commands and obeys them, he is the one who loves me. He who loves me will be loved by my Father, and I too will love him and show myself to him." Love is proven through action and not words. That is why our obedience displays our love and reverence for God.

The verses here are very clear that we are to work for wages so we can make an honest and wholehearted effort to support our families and ourselves. God encourages the hard worker and blesses his efforts. He gives everyone a marketable skill in order to gain income—contracting, accounting, law enforcement, office managers—the list is endless. But the point is that we have all been given the ability to work so we need to do it! God certainly does not want us to become lazy or idle. This is obviously different if someone is disabled or ill. But being idle is a slap in the face to God. It is as if we were to say, "What you have given me is not good enough so I will just do nothing!"

The list of scriptures about working, laziness, slothfulness, along with employer and employee relationships, seems endless. The Bible has a great deal to say about the right way to work as an employer, as well as being an upright employee.

The central theme is that we are to work diligently with a good attitude while bringing honor to God in the workplace. The Proverbs 31 woman is a perfect example of someone who was given many gifts and abilities and used them properly according to God's economy.

Julie, a lady in Orange County, California, does all these things mentioned in the Proverbs 31 passage with a loving attitude. She partners with her husband in the company he founded and has been a major reason for their success. Together they are an incredible pair of Christians whose love for the Lord overflows into the workplace. They treat all their employees with respect and fairness. Julie has no aspirations for getting rich, but she is always striving for success. She manages her time well and knows how to balance working relationships with getting the job done right. Julie is also a wonderful wife and mother. Her husband is blessed to have such a great partner.

Now, there is a difference between working hard and being a workaholic. Workaholics are rarely respected in the workplace because they are seen as people with limited free time and unhealthy tunnel vision. They cannot seem to balance relationships with their job because their priorities are all out of whack. The workaholic becomes overtired and run down, his efficiency is compromised, his colleagues become irritated, and his family suffers. This is definitely not what God wanted when he gave this person his abilities. Regardless of our jobs or family situations, we all have twenty-four hours in a day and should prioritize them wisely.

The *kind* of work and service we produce says a lot about our faith. God's Word requires Christians to make high quality products and provide exceptional service. This reflects our relationship with Christ and demonstrates our value system when we work hard and do what we say we will during employment. The Lord is not honored by anything less than fairness and concern for others including our relationship with employers/employees, competitors, and government officials who monitor businesses.

Sometimes we do not see the direct results of our hard work until much later in life. For instance, stay-at-home moms do not have a pension plan or a paycheck to vouch for their efforts, but their hard work is rewarded when their children grow up learning the important lessons they need for life and godliness. Regardless of whether we see the fruit of our labor presently or in the distant future, we are still called to work with our hands to earn a living.

As we move forward, let's keep in mind that as stewards of the Most High God we must be able to differentiate between what the world calls good management and what the Bible says to do in the economy of God. Faithful management is unselfish ambition for the sake of Christ, whereas the world teaches us to be competitive for our own goals.

We must be ambitious for the Lord. There is certainly nothing wrong with trying to make your way in the world by striving for excellence, but that perseverance must be accompanied by a heart eager to serve God. For example, pushing through medical school can be very demanding; but if the student is earning his degree because he feels the Lord is calling him as a caregiver to the sick, his task is a very noble one! It is the same in every position. Striving through a dental hygienist's program or learning construction can be tedious, but if you have a mind to use those talents to serve in God's kingdom, continue persevering! These workers have godly ambition because their hearts are centered on bringing God glory.

On the flip side, doing things out of selfish ambition will lead us nowhere. We will only receive rewards of frustration and misery. "But if you have bitter jealously and selfish ambition in your heart, do not be arrogant and so lie against the truth. This wisdom is not that which comes down from above but is earthly, natural, demonic. For where jealously and selfish ambition exist, there is disorder and every evil thing" (James 3:14-16). Certainly we can see that the outlook for doing things for ourselves is not promising.

Consider this verse as an encouragement. "We also have as our ambition…to be pleasing to Him. For we must all appear before the judgment seat of Christ so, that each one may be recompensed for his deeds" (2 Corinthians 5:9-10). What is inside one's heart motivates what comes out! What we do for God is a result of our values, feelings, beliefs, and relationship with Christ. Even though this has been said many times, God knows what the attitude of our heart. If we do something for ourselves disguised as servant's work, He knows it really is not.

Stewardship starts in the heart and ends in obedient action. The only antidote to this is to check and recheck our motives.

Prayer of Change

Lord, thank you for my ability to work. Thank you for the gifts and talents you have given me to earn a living while I honor you. Father, prevent me from becoming lazy or overambitious in my work. Keep me from giving in to job apathy or the workaholic syndrome. Teach me how to prioritize and balance my activities. Jesus, bring people into my life that can keep me accountable. I ask for your grace to maximize my efforts for you. In Jesus' name I pray. Amen.

FUTURE PLANNING

Economic Principle:
being prepared.

In the house of the wise are stores of choice food and oil, but a foolish man devours all he has. Proverbs 21:20

There is no wisdom, no insight, no plan that can succeed against the LORD. Proverbs 21:30

A prudent man sees danger and takes refuge, but the simple keep going and suffer for it. Proverbs 22:3

Now let's move to our next economic principle. Proverbs 21:20 states that "In the house of the wise are stores of choice food and oil, but a foolish man devours all he has." Verse 30 continues more blatantly that, "there is no wisdom, no insight, no plan that can succeed against the Lord."

The principle here is that a steward should plan for the future. He should not hoard, but carefully save over time so when an emergency comes along, he is prepared. In God's economy we cannot just take things as they come. We prepare for what we can and trust God to provide the rest. Verse 30 continues with the clear warning that not following the Lord's ways never ends beneficially. There is simply no use in concocting a plan if it does not follow the Lord's commands. It is vital to align both our hearts and lives with His Word.

Good stewardship also implies saying no to pledging, giving, and co-signing when we know it could come back to haunt us later. I know a dad who cosigned with his son on a car loan, believing his son would make the payments on time. Things went all right in the beginning, but then the son fell behind and eventually the car was repossessed and the father's credit suffered in the process. Perhaps the father was a little too trusting of his teenage son, and obviously the son was unfaithful in his duties. The moral of the story is that being a good steward requires serious contemplation before entering into an agreement of any kind. Generally we want to help our friends, family, and children learn to make it on their own, or help them in a time of need, but we must be careful not to let emotions overshadow prudence.

Stewardship is all about the faithful administration of the time, talents, and treasures God has given us. We are to put them to use in every area of our lives so that everyone can experience the love of Christ flowing through us. We are administrators, stewards, managers, judges, counselors, encouragers, providers, worshipers, and teachers. In a word: vessels. We are instruments created to carry out God's glorifying work, and far be it from us to impede His precious process!

Prayer of Change

Almighty Creator, I trust that you will provide me with everything I need. But as I trust you, help me to learn the balance of preparing for the future and leaving things in your hands. Father, it is so easy to get caught up in the "doing" of things, so I ask that you remind me through your Word to keep a level head. I pray this in Jesus' name. Amen.

Examples of Stewardship

Economic Principle:
learning from the life of Joseph.

Joseph's master took him and put him in prison, the place where the king's prisoners were confined. But while Joseph was there in the prison, the LORD was with him; he showed him kindness and granted him favor in the eyes of the prison warden. So the warden put him in charge of all those in the prison, and he was made responsible for all that was done there. Genesis 39:20-22

And now let Pharaoh look for a discerning and wise man and put him in charge of the land of Egypt. Let Pharaoh appoint commissioners over the land to take a fifth of the harvest of Egypt during the seven years of abundance. They should collect all the food of these good years that are coming and store up the grain under the authority of Pharaoh, to be kept in the cities for food. This food should be held in reserve for the country, to be used during the seven years of famine that will come upon Egypt, so that the country may not be ruined by the famine.
The plan seemed good to Pharaoh and to all of his officials. So Pharaoh asked them, "Can we find anyone like this man, one in whom is the spirit of God?" Then Pharaoh said to Joseph, "Since God has made all this known to you, there is no one as discerning and wise as you. You shall be in charge of my palace, and all my people are to submit to your orders. Only with respect to

115

*the throne will I be greater than you." So Pharaoh said
to Joseph, "I hereby put you in charge of the whole land
of Egypt."* Genesis 41:33-41

*When the famine had spread over the whole country,
Joseph opened the storehouses and sold grain to the
Egyptians, for the famine was severe throughout Egypt.
And all the countries came to Egypt to buy grain from
Joseph, because the famine was severe in all the world.*
Genesis 41:56-57

What a great story! After all that happened to Joseph, God put him in charge of prisons and a whole kingdom! That is an amazing miracle that only God could have performed!

Joseph was a manager and steward. The Lord lifted him up from the pit his brothers threw him in and made him governor of Egypt. Joseph had a strong, moral character that helped him succeed, but it was the Lord who did the blessing.

Joseph's leadership saved his country from starvation. He did not lord his lofty position over the people by withholding grain, but he also did not forsake his position as an employee. He sold food to make a profit, but did not dominate the other countries. He made the king proud.

Let us remember that God alone controls our affairs and plans, as He did with Joseph's. Our role is to be obedient and loving to God in character. But let us learn that Joseph was a great steward because he managed carefully what did not belong to him. It was not his own private property, but he cared for it as though it were. He was a faithful servant. His employer was pleased. Do we rightly honor our employers?

Whatever we do, let us be wise managers of what does not belong to us. Joseph's witness was on display, and thankfully it was a good witness. Our testimony is constantly being scrutinized and imitated as well. Let's make sure it is a good one! Let's bring glory to God by being faithful employees, even when no one is watching.

We also need to plan ahead. Joseph had a plan to save up for the hard times he knew were coming. Do we think that because our income is good now that it will always be plentiful? We put ourselves in a more secure position when we save for an emergency. Joseph was prepared. Are we?

Economic Principle:
learning from the life of Daniel.

It pleased Darius to appoint 120 satraps to rule throughout the kingdom, with three administrators over them, one of them who was Daniel. The satraps were made accountable to them so that the king might not suffer loss. Now Daniel so distinguished himself among the administrators and the satraps by his exceptional qualities that the king planned to set him over the whole kingdom. At this, the administrators and the satraps tried to find charges against Daniel in his conduct of government affairs, but they were unable to do so. They could find no corruption in him, because he was trustworthy and neither corrupt nor negligent. Daniel 6:1-4

Daniel was a faithful and unwavering man in both his professional and personal life. He was one of the three officials who oversaw the other 120. He was a very powerful yet humble steward, never using his power for selfish gain. Daniel's character was trustworthy enough that his fellow colleagues could find no flaw in him. When they set traps to catch him in an unlawful act, their own plans foiled against them because of his integrity.

King Darius knew of Daniel's uprightness as well, and revered him as his most trusted employee. Even when he was forced to throw Daniel into the lion's den due to a deceptive law, he begged that Daniel's God would save him from certain death. Daniel's integrity as a true steward of God was so unyielding that he was faithful even to an unjust death! However, the Lord saved Daniel from being eaten alive and His name was glorified all the more when the king acknowledged that "every part of [his] kingdom must fear and reverence the God of Daniel." What an awesome testimony Daniel was for his Lord.

Prayer of Change

Almighty God, help me to remember that your hand is on me always, in unfair and favorable times. You alone control my events and circumstances. Help me to be wise in management, giving, and saving, so that I can honor you and bless others. Like Joseph, let me be faithful in all situations and not complain or blame you in bad times. Lord, help me not to withhold from others in need, but be generous for all I have comes from you, Almighty God; you provide for me. In Jesus' name I pray. Amen.

SEEKING COUNSEL

Economic Principle:
looking for good advice before making a decision.

Listen to advice and accept instruction, and in the end you will be wise. Proverbs 19:20

The way of a fool seems right to him, but the wise man listens to advice. Proverbs 12:15

I will praise the LORD who counsels me. Psalm 16:7

Plans fail for lack of counsel, but with many advisers they succeed. Proverbs 15:22

A simple man believes anything, but a prudent man gives thought to his steps. Proverbs 14:15

For waging war you need guidance, and for victory many advisers. Proverbs 24:6

Listen to advice and accept instruction, and in the end you will be wise. Proverbs 19:20

It is better to heed a wise man's rebuke than to listen to the song of fools. Ecclesiastes 7:5

O how I love your law! It is my meditation all the day. Your commandments make me wiser than my enemies, for they are ever mine. I have more insight than all my teachers, for your testimonies are my meditation. I understand more than the aged, because I have observed your precepts. I have restrained my feet from every evil way, that I may keep your word. I have not turned aside from your ordinances, for you yourself have taught me. How sweet are your words to my taste! Yes, sweeter than honey to my mouth! From your precepts I get under-standing; therefore I hate every false way. Psalm 119:97-104

These verses point out that there is simply too much to know when it comes to stewardship. Dealing with money is overwhelming to any one person. Nobody can know every-thing about estate planning, insurance, taxes, and the many other areas of finance. This is why there are areas of specializa-tion. Because God's Word commands us to seek godly counsel before making a decision, we can look for help with a clear conscience. We must leave our egos at the door and be willing to listen to the advice we seek, or else our efforts are futile.

In God's economy, things are not always easy. Who wants to hear a rebuke or be reproved? It certainly is not fun, but it is valuable. Think of the pain and suffering avoided by listen-ing to wise counsel. Sometimes we have to eat a little humble pie and accept the help of others with matters we do not know about.

Proverbs 27:23-24 says, "Be sure you know the condition of your flocks, give careful attention to your herds; for riches do not endure forever, and a crown is not secure for all gener-ations." A good steward knows what is going on. The steward knows where everything is located, whether or not it needs to be replaced soon, and its value. He is keenly aware of the con-dition of *all* property because he purposefully pays attention. It is his job!

This idea should remind us of the afore mentioned verse in Luke 16:10-12,

"Whoever can be trusted with very little can also be trusted with much, and whoever is dishonest with very little will also be dishonest with much. So if you have not been trustworthy in handling worldly wealth, who will trust you with true riches? And if you have not been trustworthy with someone else's property, who will give you property of your own?"

It does not matter if the responsibility is great or small; Jesus is telling each of us believers how to enrich ourselves with spiritual blessings. He is teaching us to value the development of our character as He does. As stewards awaiting our heavenly rewards, we want to prove faithful in whatever the Lord has called us to do. This principle does not just hold true in our career or professional life, but in our personal life as well. First Timothy 5:8 says that, "If anyone does not provide for his relatives, and especially for his immediate family, he has denied the faith and is worse than an unbeliever." If we do not carry out our duties with the people we love most, why would we be inclined to do so with strangers? So whether our job is being a plumber or a stay-at-home mom, we must invest everything we have into doing our best. If we work part-time or are on disability, the command is still the same: be faithful.

Do not be the kind of Christian who loves to give advice, but doesn't take it when it is his turn to listen. All of us could use some help in at least one area or another; so don't be afraid to ask for help! The Web site www.Crown.org is a great place to obtain godly financial advice. Here are some categories that would be good to look into:

1. Real estate
2. Accounting
3. Wills/trusts
4. Insurance agents
5. Financial planning
6. Investments
7. Loans and mortgages
8. Risk management
9. Business/self-employment consultants
10. Bank/credit union advisers

Refusing godly counsel is a sin. As stewards of God, we must call upon the gifted in the areas we are not qualified in. If we know we can be more effective for God but won't take the necessary steps because of our pride, we are managing God's resources poorly. Refusing help, or being apathetic towards it, stunts our growth as believers. We will continue walking around in the same stagnant circle as before, just wasting time and resources. Help is available for everything under the sun, so seek advice. This is our responsibility!

Prayer of Change

Heavenly Father, I understand that it is best to seek counsel before making a decision. I admit that I have not always done that. Jesus, sometimes it is hard for me to accept other people's help, so teach me to have a humble spirit so I can glean from these godly advisors. I pray this in Jesus' name. Amen.

INVESTING

Economic Principle: preparing for the future.

"Which one of you, when he wants to build a tower, does first not sit down and calculate the cost, to see if he has enough to complete it? Otherwise, when he has laid a foundation, and is not able to finish, all who observe it begin to ridicule him, saying, 'This man began to build and was not able to finish.'" Luke 14:28-30

"The wise man saves for the future, but the foolish man spends whatever he gets." Proverbs 21:20

"Steady plodding brings prosperity; hasty speculation brings poverty." Proverbs 21:5

"Cast your bread upon the waters, for after many days you will find it again. Give portions to seven, yes to eight, for you do now what disaster may come upon the land." Ecclesiastes 11:1-2

As we continue forward, a good steward learns investing. We know that part of having a surplus is to make the sum grow for future use. To invest is to further God's kingdom, His ultimate purpose, and the Great Commission. As in the parable of the talents, we invest God's resources so that the distribution and return will be greater than just sticking the money in the ground as the wicked servant did.

A good and faithful steward diversifies. Diversification is a wise investment tool and also reduces risk. If an unexpected problem should strike one particular investment, the other assets can pick up the slack. These different investments increase chances of a greater overall return. Ecclesiastes wisely admonishes us to "give portions to seven, yes to eight, for you do not know what disaster may come upon the land" (11:2). This verse gives us the "go ahead" to invest and see how God may work. Obviously, we must not throw our money around frivolously and gamble with the Almighty's resources, but we must calculate the cost and plan how we may go about obtaining our particular venture.

Ask yourself the question Jesus asked: "Which one of you, when he wants to build a tower, does not first sit down and calculate the cost, to see if he has enough to complete it?" Mull over the particulars, talk to your spouse, seek financial advice, and, most importantly, pray before continuing on; then go!

For the believers reading this book, most of us can remember the time and place we gave our life to Christ. Maybe we were youngsters in Sunday school or teenagers in a Bible study, or perhaps the sins of our past weighed us down as adults and we ran to Christ for freedom. Regardless of when or where we came to Christ, we all had to count the cost. We may not have been thinking about it at the time, but if our heart was right and we truly believed Jesus took our spot on the cross for our sins, we soon realized there was a cost involved in following Christ. In other countries where Christians are martyred and Bibles are forbidden, the cost of following Christ is much more life-threatening. But genuine believers all over the world have experienced the discipline and denial it takes to crucify that sinful nature on the cross. This is the precious message we are entrusted with as stewards. Are we sharing the gospel in the workplace? Are we actively inviting people to church? If an unbeliever we knew suddenly died, could we rest assured that we had done our duty to tell him the good news?

The Lord never promised us an easy life as Christians. In fact, Jesus says that "all men will hate you because of me" (Matthew 10:22). But does that mean we should shy away from the challenge? Honestly, whose opinion do we care more about: God's or man's? It *should* be the former, but sadly, in most cases it is the latter. The gospel is the most treasured gift we could give to anyone, no matter how it is received. Thus, if we are going to practice any area of stewardship, let it be this one!

Prayer of Change

Dear Lord, I don't want to shy away from a challenge that you want to use to grow my character. I understand that sometimes I will have to go out on a limb and just simply trust you. Lord, I also understand that investing is not just a financial issue. I want to invest in godly things like sharing the gospel and teaching my children to love you. Father, I need help in figuring out the best things to invest in. Please give me the ability to discern in these areas. I praise you for what you are currently doing in my life! In Jesus' name. Amen.

RISK MANAGEMENT

Economic Principle:
assessing potential hazards.

A prudent man sees evil and hides himself, the naïve proceed and pay the penalty. Proverbs 27:12

A prudent man sees danger and takes refuge, but the simple keep going and suffer for doing it. Proverbs 22:3

Be shrewd as serpents and innocent as doves. Matthew 10:16

Which one of you, when he wants to build a tower, does not first sit down and calculate the cost, to see if he has enough to complete it? Otherwise, when he has laid a foundation and is not able to finish, all who observe it begin to ridicule him, saying, "This man began to build and was not able to finish." Luke 14:28-30

In God's economy, it is vital to protect oneself as a part of wise management and in regards to personal stewardship. Managing investments and paying appropriate taxes are also parts of stewardship, but we will take a closer look at these issues later. For now we will look at the need for insurance and risk management.

As we saw from the verses mentioned earlier, foreseeing trouble ahead of time and managing it properly are important aspects of stewardship. In God's economy, we need to protect ourselves *before* the problem happens.

Whether we are single or married, insurance is a wise method of protection. The economic principle is not replacing our faith in God with human institutions by purchasing every insurance policy available, but rather guarding yourself against potential problems according to the means you have available. The Bible says to be shrewd, watchful, and prudent. For example, if you own a house on a hill where it rains often, it would be wise to buy flood and mudslide insurance. If your teenage son is learning how to drive, it is prudent—and necessary—to buy a policy that covers *all* the cars. Health insurance is almost mandatory, and if cancer runs in your family, buying a specific policy to cover those expenses might not be such a bad idea. These are just a few examples of how to guard against the unexpected future. This, of course, does not eliminate our need to trust our Savior; it simply reaffirms it.

Theoretically, someone could self-insure if he had enough saved up, but few families have that kind of money. It is best to have auto, home, health, and life insurance to cover all the main avenues in our lives. The most common disasters include car accidents, heart disease, cancer, and natural disasters. The above types of insurances should cover all these areas.

Prayer of Change

Lord, you are whom I trust. I know that you have given me the ability to guard against danger, so I ask your guidance in helping me decide how to best protect my family. Give me wisdom in how to apply the truth of your Word to the stewardship area of my life. I pray this in Jesus' name. Amen.

FAITHFULNESS

Economic Principle:
being obedient and persevering to do good.

*So then, men ought to regard us as servants of Christ
and as those entrusted with the secret things of God.
Now it is required that those who have been given a
trust must prove faithful.* 1 Corinthians 4:1-2

Faithfulness involved in stewardship involves hard work.
We are employed by our heavenly Father to do the best
job we can. We can all admit that there are many times we have
not given 100 percent at the office or factory. Maybe we have
taken an extra long break, called in sick when we really felt
fine, or shoved our responsibilities off on someone else. In
some way, we have taken the easy way out.

If we want to see results in the workplace or reach a new
level of performance, we have to put in our time and effort.
The farmer does not sit and watch his land expectantly wait-
ing for corn to just pop up. He first plants the seeds, tills the
land, and makes sure the soil has all the nutrients it needs. The
same principle can be applied to God's economy. Stewardship
must be practiced every day and given special attention. It
must be pruned, watered, and fed just like a plant. Being a
good steward means recognizing frivolous efforts and not
wasting time or money with the Lord's resources. We've
already looked at the examples of Joseph and Daniel. They
were faithful to the Lord and His work even when they were
harassed and treated unfairly. They never compromised their
beliefs or convictions, even when their very life was in danger.

How do we measure up with these guys? When we are all alone like Daniel, do we bow to pray? When we are betrayed by family and friends like Joseph, do we continue worshiping the Lord for His sovereignty? The point is that faithfulness is being obediently reverent when no eye but God's is on us. Faithfulness is persevering under trial and continuing to do good. Discipline is not easy, but it is required of us as believers and as stewards.

Prayer of Change

Father God, I know I have some faithfulness issues. Sometimes I start things and don't finish them. Other times I say I'm going to do something and I never follow through. Jesus, I know that you are a faithful God, and you have shown me that characteristic, not only in the way you deal with me but also in the examples you have given me to pattern my life after. Please remind me how I can me more faithful in my day-to-day activities. In Jesus' name. Amen.

Taxes

Economic Principle:
giving to Caesar what is Caesar's.

Keeping a close watch on him, they sent spies, who pretended to be honest. They hoped to catch Jesus in something he said so that they might hand him over to the power and authority of the governor. So the spies questioned him: "Teacher, we know that you speak and teach what is right, and that you do not show partiality but teach the way of God in accordance with the truth. Is it right for us to pay taxes to Caesar or not?" He saw through their duplicity and said to them, "Show me a denarius. Whose portrait and inscription are on it?" "Caesar's," they replied. He said to them, "Then give to Caesar what is Caesar's, and to God what is God's."
Luke 20:20-25

"No servant can serve two masters. Either he will hate the one and love the other, or he will be devoted to the one and despise the other. You cannot serve both God and Money." The Pharisees, who loved money, heard all this and were sneering at Jesus. He said to them, "You are the ones who justify yourselves in the eyes of men, but God knows your hearts. What is highly valued among men is detestable in God's sight." Luke 16:13-14

Because of this you also pay taxes, for rulers are servants of God, devoting themselves to this very thing. Render to all what is due them: tax to whom tax is due; custom to whom custom; fear to whom fear; honor to whom honor. Romans 13:6-7

While we are on the topic, it is imperative to mention the importance of paying taxes. Some people think that working "under the table" or not reporting all their income is a way of saving money. On the contrary, it stops God's generous flow of abundance on our lives because it is a sin. Romans 13:6-7 states very clearly that we are to "render to all what is due them, tax to whom tax is due, custom to whom custom, fear to whom fear, honor to whom honor."

Paying taxes is important not only for its monetary value but because of the principle it holds. It both acknowledges and honors the authorities above us: mayors, governors, presidents, and God. We set a godly example for others, and we obey the King of kings.

God's economy is not a cafeteria plan where we can pick and choose what rules to abide by. Just as we have already learned with the other principles in this book, it is all about having an obedient heart that glorifies God. Do not let cutting taxes or penny-pinching be the number one governing principle in your life. Luke 16:13-14 says that "No servant can serve two masters. Either he will hate the one and love the other, or he will be devoted to the one and despise the other. You cannot serve both God and money." The love of money not only sets you outside of God's presence, but it is the root of all different kinds of evil as well.

It is very easy to know if money is more important than the Lord:

1. Are you consumed with earning money?
2. Do you count every penny?

3. Are you always looking for ways to save money—to a fault?

4. Do you constantly stress over the numbers in your checkbook?

5. Do you find yourself thinking about money in your spare time?

6. Do you withhold tithe?

7. Do you withhold gifts to others?

8. Are you harboring bitterness towards God for not improving your financial position?

These are just a few questions you can ask yourself. If you answered yes to any of the above questions, there is a good chance that money is master in your life. The options following this understanding are clear: Change your habits with money immediately by asking for God's forgiveness, grace, and guidance, or continue serving your own god and suffer the consequences of living outside of God's presence.

Leave it to Christ to say it like it is! He leaves no room for misinterpretation. There is absolutely no toleration for apathy. In Revelation 3:16 God says that "Because you are lukewarm, and neither hot nor cold, I will spit you out of My mouth." No tepid water, fence balancing, or teeter-tottering will be allowed for a child of God.

Prayer of Change

Dear Lord, I want to honor you in all the financial areas of my life. I realize that I have missed the mark already. Jesus, please forgive me for being dishonest. Lord, I don't want to waver on what is right or wrong, but to simply do what I know is correct. Fill me with an over-whelming desire to please and glorify you. Let me be absolutely on fire for you in finances, my relationships, and all the other areas of my life! I pray this in Jesus' name. Amen.

CHEATING AND STEALING

Economic Principle: exchanging the truth for a lie.

Food gained by fraud tastes sweet to a man, but he ends up with a mouth full of gravel. Proverbs 20:17

In being responsible servants of God, we must not have the characteristics of cheating and stealing. That may seem obvious, but in some countries where human trafficking and slavery still exist, this verse is appropriate.

For those who buy and sell people like a commodity, only pain and judgment will result. It surely is not anything new. From the beginning of time, people have been bought and sold for financial gain, but that certainly does not nullify the fact that it is sin.

Another popular and satanic business in our world today is fortune-telling. These psychics tell untrue stories and give false hopes to people hungry to hear what they want. What is worse, Satan is worshiped outright, and even summoned for guidance. How evil!

Many practices taste sweet in the beginning, but Proverbs 16:25 promises they will leave a bitter taste in the mouth for all eternity. Do not think about how it "feels" to you because your mind will do its best to justify why you should do or have a certain thing. Instead, focus on the facts. Classify the action according to what the Word of God calls it. If it is sin, do not try to sugarcoat it. That will only leave you deceived, delirious, and destined for destruction.

Cheating and stealing can also come in simpler forms, like cheating on a test or taking supplies from work that we didn't pay for. The reason these things are called sin is because they shun honesty. God is the Father of all truth and He cannot stand a lie. Cheating on a test is like saying, "I deserve this grade because this is my work" when in reality it isn't. Even taking things without asking can be considered stealing because it means avoiding telling the truth or hiding another sneaky agenda we may have. Cheating and stealing directly contradict God's character. If we are going to call ourselves children of God, we cannot participate in this kind of behavior.

Prayer of Change

Father God, I admit that I have cheated and stolen from you and from others. I recognize that this is like lying. I want to be honest in all my dealings, so please help me to value honestly above anything else. Help me to resist the temptation that might encourage me to take the easy way out. I pray this in Jesus' name. Amen.

BANKRUPTCY

Economic Principle:
the result of a tragic borrowing game.

The wicked borrow and do not repay, but the righteous give generously. Psalm 37:21

If a man borrows anything from his neighbor, and it is injured or dies while its owner is not with it, he shall make full restitution. If its owner is with it, he shall not make restitution; if it is hired, it came for its hire. Exodus 22:14-15

The alien who is among you shall rise above you higher and higher, but you shall go down lower and lower. He shall lend to you, but you shall not lend to him; he shall be the head, and you shall be the tail. So all these curses shall come on you and pursue you and overtake you until you are destroyed, because you would not obey the LORD your God by keeping His commandments and His statutes which He commanded you. Deuteronomy 28:43-45

The rich rules over the poor, and the borrower becomes the lender's slave. Proverbs 22:7

The people will be like the priest, the servant like his master, the maid like her mistress, the buyer like the seller, the lender like the borrower, the creditor like the debtor. Isaiah 24:2

If you lend money to My people, to the poor among you, you are not to act as a creditor to him; you shall not charge him interest. Exodus 22:25

He does not put out his money at interest, nor does he take a bribe against the innocent. He who does these things will never be shaken. Psalm 15:5

Do not be among those who give pledges, among those who become guarantors for debts. If you have nothing with which to pay, why should he take your bed from under you? Proverbs 22:26-27

He who increases his wealth by interest and usury, gathers it for him who is gracious to the poor. Proverbs 28:8

"If a man does not oppress anyone, but restores to the debtor his pledge, does not commit robbery, but gives his bread to the hungry and covers the naked with clothing, if he does not lend money on interest or take increase, if he keeps his hand from iniquity and executes true justice between man and man, if he walks in My statutes and My ordinances so as to deal faithfully—he is righteous and will surely live," declares the Lord GOD....
"[If he] oppresses the poor and needy, commits robbery, does not restore a pledge, but lifts up his eyes to the idols, and commits abomination, he lends money on interest and takes increase; will he live? He will not live! He has committed all these abominations, he will surely be put to death; his blood will be on his own head."...
"[He does not] oppress anyone, or retain a pledge, or commit robbery, but he gives his bread to the hungry and covers

the naked with clothing, he keeps his hand from the poor, does not take interest or increase, but executes My ordinances, and walks in My statutes; he will not die for his father's iniquity, he will surely live. As for his father, because he practiced extortion, robbed his brother and did what was not good among his people, behold, he will die for his iniquity." Ezekiel 18:7-9,12-13,16-18

All day long he is gracious and lends, and his descendants are a blessing. Psalm 37:26

It is well with the man who is gracious and lends; he will maintain his cause in judgment. Psalm 112:5

Give to him who asks of you, and do not turn away from him who wants to borrow from you. Matthew 5:42

If you lend to those from whom you expect to receive, what credit is that to you? Even sinners lend to sinners, in order to receive back the same amount. But love your enemies, and do good, and lend, expecting nothing in return; and your reward will be great, and you will be sons of the Most High; for He Himself is kind to ungrateful and evil men. Luke 6:34-35

Will not all of these take up a taunt-song against him, even mockery and insinuations against him, and say, "Woe to him who increases what is not his—for how long—and makes himself rich with loans? Will not your creditors rise up suddenly, and those who collect awaken? Indeed, you will become plunder for them."
Habakkuk 2:6-7

Do not withhold good from those to whom it is due, when it is in your power to do it. Do not say to your neighbor, "Go, and come back, and tomorrow I will give it," when you have it with you. Proverbs 3:27-28

Make friends quickly with your opponent at law while you are with him on the way, so that your opponent may not hand you over to the judge, and the judge to the officer, and you shall be thrown into prison. Truly I say to you, you shall not come out of there until you have paid up the last cent. Matthew 5:25-26

Owe nothing to anyone except to love one another; for he who loves his neighbor has fulfilled the law. Romans 13:8

If he has wronged you in any way, or owes you anything, charge that to my account; I, Paul, am writing this with my own hand, I will repay it. Philemon 1:18-19

A man lacking in sense pledges and becomes guarantor in the presence of his neighbor. Proverbs 17:18

He who is guarantor for a stranger will surely suffer for it, but he who refuses to strike hands in pledge is safe. Proverbs 11:15

Let the creditor seize all that he has, and let strangers plunder the product of his labor. Psalm 109:11

Bankruptcy is a huge issue in God's economy. Not only is it detrimental to one's financial position, but more often than not, it ruins relationships. Bankruptcy is a borrowing game that has gotten out of control. We can be in debt to a credit card company, a bank, or even our own parents. Being unable to repay these obligations puts undue strain on a relationship that usually leads to its ultimate demise. In this book, we want to learn how to restore these situations and how to prevent them in the first place.

Those who borrow and do not repay are labeled "wicked." The Bible says that it is stealing, and we all know that stealing is a violation of one of God's Ten Commandments. This includes anyone who does not intend to repay the money he borrowed. God's economic principle is that if we borrow, we should promptly repay. Sometimes special circumstances arise such as emergencies, medical issues, or job-related cutbacks, but God wants us to make a solid attempt at returning the money. If we do, He will bless our efforts.

It is not a sin to borrow, but it is a sin not to return it. Even if one spends his entire life paying back the debt, it is still a necessary action that God commands. We are to keep our promises.

We are also not to become responsible for another's debt. When a person becomes legally liable for the debt, default, or failure in duty of another, it is called surety. We are obligated for someone else's debt if we helped him get a loan and he cannot pull through. Even if our intentions were meant to help him, we take a risk when we sign our name.

It is not the money or business the Lord is worried about. He could have an infinite number of those if He wanted. He cares about the strain debt inflicts on relationships. Marriages often collapse under financial pressures, and friendships also dry up when money becomes an issue. Not only borrowing and money-related issues, but anything that sets itself up between God's glory and improving human relationships is an impediment in a Christian's growth.

We in the United States have perverted the use of borrowing and credit to a terrible degree. We borrow money for houses, cars, education, and whatever else suits our fancy. And as this behavior continues, we move ourselves closer and closer to bankruptcy. If someone has declared bankruptcy, he has God's forgiveness to rest in if he has repented, but before reaching that point he must make every effort he can to repay. Even after bankruptcy has been declared, the utmost integrity is demonstrated when one tries to make restitution—to credit card companies, family members, the IRS, government school loan agencies, friends, and other creditors.

The concept we need to understand is that God sees our heart and our intentions. He knows whether or not we are putting forth our best effort. He knows if we are being lazy or if we are exhausted in our efforts. Nothing is hidden from the Lord.

Churches are not exempt from this biblical principle either; in fact, they are even more accountable because they are examples to the individuals within its walls. Churches in debt are horrible examples of stewardship. We would much rather have our money going to youth programs, missions, and other ministries where it is supposed to go, than to an interest payment on debt, would we not?

As Christians, we are the light of the world. Maybe they do not want to admit it, but the world looks to us as models of correct behavior. What are we teaching them when we are in debt? Worse, what are we saying when we do not pay back the money? We are simply showing them that our word carries no weight and cannot be trusted. The Bible goes to great lengths to teach us to be slow in making vows because if we are unable to keep them, it shames us. When we say "yes," people should be able to trust that it will happen, and similarly when we say "no." This is what James meant when he said in 5:12, "Let your 'Yes' be yes, and your 'No,' no, or you will be condemned."

God prefers us to be lenders rather than borrowers. Even if we lend money and the debtor is unable to pay us back, we have the option to forgive the debt, an action that is very liberating and followed by a blessing from the Lord. Anyone who is currently in debt and wants to take steps towards re-creating a plausible budget can visit Crown Ministries at www.crown.org for a free financial adviser. There *are* options out there, and if you have been looking for some sign for help, consider these words to be flashing neon.

Prayer of Change

Father God, help me to repay what I borrow and to honor others, even if I do not know them. Help me to look out for their best interests. Help me to repay my bills in a timely manner and to demonstrate integrity in my finances.

Lord, please prevent me from borrowing in the future. Search my heart to find the secret sins that may cause me to end up in financial bondage. Lord, guide me in applying the truth of your Word practically in my everyday life. In addition, remind me to come to you first when I am in need. Perhaps through prayer and patience I can give you an opportunity to provide instead of borrowing. I pray this all in Jesus' name. Amen.

One Body, Many Members

Economic Principle:
we are all individuals with different gifts
called to work together to honor God.

Who are you to judge someone else's servant? To his own master [God] he stands or falls. Romans 14:4

Just as each of us has one body with many members, and these members do not all have the same function, so in Christ we who are many form one body, and each member belongs to all the others. We have different gifts according to the grace given us. If a man's gift is prophesying, let him use it in proportion to his faith. If it is serving, let him serve; if it is teaching, let him teach. If it is encouraging, let him encourage; if it is contributing to the needs of others, let him give generously; if it is leadership, let him govern diligently; if it is showing mercy, let him do it cheerfully. Romans 12:4-8

Everyone has different functions and purposes based on what God has given them to do, yet we all work in a unified body with the common goal of bringing Jesus glory. This is not a baseball team where everyone is the pitcher! Who would catch the ball? And just as the first baseman is not ranked higher than the shortstop, so God does not rank us according to our abilities. We are all essential pieces to the puzzle. The encourager is not less important than the teacher. Without him, where would the teacher receive his encouragement?

If we all focused on our own talents without understanding how they help each other, this would cause divisiveness and resentment between fellow believers. Satan would love for us to work selfishly because then we would be less effective. Refusing to be a part of God's team or even just becoming apathetic towards working together only gives the devil the upper hand.

The best way we can be an effective steward in the church setting is to seek out a position where our spiritual gift will be used. A person with the gift of teaching might seek a Sunday school position, those with the gift of administration can work in the office, and encouragers can counsel people with special needs. These are just a few examples, but there are many needs that are necessary to fill. So if you are not already serving in a capacity that you like and are good at, look for one. The elders of your church will be glad to help you with this.

Earlier, we talked about the parable of the talents and how there will eventually be an accounting for our efforts on earth. These efforts, we learned, do not include our money only, but our time, talents, relationships, power and authority, our bodies, and even the teaching of God's Word to others. James 3:1 states, "Let not many of you become teachers, my brethren, knowing that as such we will incur a stricter judgment." God imposes different levels and standards on His children for the managing of different gifts and situations. He is the one who decides what standards of accountability apply to His people, and His Word illustrates these concepts that must be taken seriously.

Human nature being innately evil, and without an accounting or final judgment, people would not have a deterrent for poor management. How many of us would desire to follow God without some kind of punishment or reward system? Romans 3:10 says that none of us are good and none of us would seek God without Him first calling us. The "it-does-not-matter" philosophy would set in and we would simply do as we please, realizing we had become our own authority. But in order to establish His sovereign authority the Lord inspired Romans 14:4, "Who are you to judge the servant of another. To his own master he stands or falls; and he will stand, for the Lord is able to make him stand."

All must stand before God on the same level as another. No one has more or less of an advantage based on wealth or ethnicity. God will demand an equal accounting from all. Because He does not play favorites, His perfect system of judgment will be partial to no one.

We cannot criticize another for what we feel is not right because that would be like playing God with the authority we know only *He* has. Judging only causes divisiveness in the body and an increase in our prideful ego—two things we definitely do not need.

Different views on stewardship can really take a toll on a marriage, and this is the institution where teamwork matters the most. Satan loves to use the issue of money to divide couples and send their marriage toward divorce. How can a wife be a good steward if her husband will not let her? What happens when he yells and screams about what she does with their money? On the other hand, how can a husband be a good steward when his wife uses allotted money for other purposes? These questions remind us how important it is to communicate with our spouse about monetary issues. Make sure you both understand each other so that each can reach his full potential as the Lord's steward. Remember, if we cannot practice a virtue at home, it certainly will not come out in public.

Here are some practical questions you can ask your mate to see if you both really do have the same view on stewardship. If you are not married, discuss these topics with your intended spouse before you take the plunge:

1. How do you define stewardship?
2. What is the source for your ideas on stewardship?
3. What kind of steward do you think I am?
4. Do I lord financial issues over you?
5. Do we have a good balance in our spending habits?
6. Are we too cheap? Extravagant?
7. Do we communicate our financial goals well?
8. What are your financial goals in the future? (retirement, college, funds)
9. How do you view our personal financial situation?
10. Do you feel we could be better managers of God's resources? How?
11. Are we instilling these principles in our kids?

Hopefully, this list will open your heart and mind to understanding one another in the arena of stewardship. It is a major blow to the devil when we allow ourselves to communicate through love in our marriages. We must first forgive each other and then refuse to bring up past arguments. God does not throw forgiven sin back in our faces, so neither should we do such a thing to others. If you and your spouse are not together in this decision, growth in your marriage will never happen. Life is a series of choices and we must be willing to live with the consequences.

Prayer of Change

Father God, understanding that I am a part of a team that aims to glorify you has improved my understanding of how I function as a believer. I want to reach my ultimate potential, not only individually but in the body of believers as well. Lord, help me to push away the thoughts that cause me to judge others or to put them down. Fill me with enthusiasm and love so that I can encourage other believers around me. I pray this in Jesus' name. Amen.

THE FINAL ACCOUNTING

Economic Principle:
all will be judged by their actions on the last day.

Each of us will give an account of himself to God.
Romans 14:12

The Lord answered, "who then is the faithful and wise manager, whom the master puts in charge of his servants to give them their food allowance at the proper time? It will be good for that servant whom the master finds doing so when he returns. I tell you the truth; he will put him in charge of all his possessions. But suppose the servant says to himself, 'My master is taking a long time coming,' and he then begins to beat the menservants and maidservants and to eat and drink and get drunk. The master of that servant will come on a day when he does not expect him and at an hour he is not aware of. He will cut him to pieces and assign him a place with the unbelievers. That servant who knows his master's will and does not get ready or does not do what his master wants will be beaten with many blows. But the one who does not know and does things deserving punishment will be beaten with few blows. From everyone who has been given much, much will be demanded; and from the one who has been entrusted with much, much more will be asked." Luke 12:42-48

Set your mind on the things above, not on the things that are on earth. Colossians 3:2

Trust in the LORD *with all your heart and lean not on your own understanding. In all your ways acknowledge Him, and He will make your paths straight.*
Proverbs 3:5-6

I have seen a grievous evil under the sun: wealth hoarded to the harm of its owner, or wealth lost through some misfortune, so that when he has a son, there is nothing left for him. Ecclesiastes 5:13-17

Whom have I in heaven but you? And earth has nothing I desire besides you. My flesh and my heart may fail, but God is the strength of my heart and my portion forever. Psalms 73:25-26

So we make it our goal to please him, whether we are at home in the body or away from it. For we must all appear before the judgment seat of Christ, that each one may receive what is due him for the things done while in the body, whether good or bad. 2 Corinthians 5:9-10

For no one can lay any foundation other than the one already laid, which is Jesus Christ. If any man builds on this foundation using gold, silver, costly stones, wood, hay, or straw, his work will be shown for what it is, because the Day will bring it to light. It will be revealed with fire, and the fire will test the quality of each man's work. If what he has built survives, he will receive his reward. If it is burned up, he will suffer loss; he himself will be saved, but only as one escaping through the flames. 1 Corinthians 3:11-15

In Luke 12:43, Jesus calls the servant "blessed" because he finds him doing as instructed when he returns. The reverse is also true for the slave who thought he could get away with his mischief while his master was gone. He was not blessed but rather condemned. Verse 46 brings the accounting for both servants. The faithful received command of all the master's possessions and the disobedient was cut to pieces and assigned a place with the unbelievers. A different level of punishment is given to him who has full knowledge of his circumstances and responsibilities, yet still chooses to disobey. So the reasoning in verse 48 is very logical. To whom much is given, much is required. God expects action from His children.

You may ask, "I was not given very much, so what is expected of me?" The answer is that you must use whatever little amount you have been given (spiritual gifts, time, and talents) for God's glory. If you are good on the computer, create a biblical Web site. If you are well-versed, write a book about a biblical issue to help others. If you have free time, volunteer at a shelter. These are just a few examples, but the idea is the same behind each opportunity: Create the means by which you can glorify God and He will bless your efforts.

To contribute to the information found in Romans and Luke, let's traverse back to the Old Testament and check out Psalms 49:16-20. We read,

> *Do not be overawed when a man grows rich, when the splendor of his house increases; for he will take nothing with him when he dies, his splendor will not descend from him. Though while he lived he counted himself blessed, and men praise you when you prosper—he will join the generation of his fathers, who will never see the*

light of life. A man who has riches without understanding is like the beasts that perish.

This passage should open our eyes to say the least. How many times have we all marveled at another's wealth? And how many times do we wonder who will inherit it? Yet in the scheme of eternity, even if we live to be 100 years old, the numbers will never come out in favor of spending so much time focused on wealth. Satan wants people to be in awe over material things because it increases their prideful greed. Their ego casts a dark shadow over what little ability they may have to see past this life. Of course, this is obviously in violation of God's economy. This philosophy is like playing with fire: Once the match is lit, it can easily catch the whole room on fire and you will be burned.

Instead of placing such high value on material objects, believers are called to value wisdom and understanding. Wisdom is being able to distinguish truth from falsehood, and understanding is applying that truth to our lives. So the truth of the matter is that we take nothing with us when we die. Applying that, we should take steps to developing character qualities rather than riches. There is no gray area here. There is no hopping the fence or wavering on top. Because God knows our hearts, at the final accounting, let's be proud we chose wisdom.

Continuing with the motif of wisdom, let's check out Ecclesiastes 7:12 which says, "Wisdom is a shelter as money is a shelter, but the advantage of knowledge is this: that wisdom preserves the life of its possessor."

Once again we see how the importance of money is downplayed while godly character qualities are prized highly. Money has limitations, meaning no matter how or where one lives, it cannot save his life. Rich men still die. Death waits for no man and money does nothing to deter it.

Solomon gives money *some* credit, saying that it can provide shelter, but a *wise* steward can also do the same thing through his wisdom: get a job, work diligently, and put a roof over his head. The wisdom discussed in this verse means to use what abilities and assets you have for God's glory. And that idea reiterates what we already learned with the Lord as the Ultimate Owner. True wisdom is relinquishing all back to Him and managing well what He leaves in our care.

Finally, let's move on to 1 Corinthians 3:11-15.

> *For no one can lay any foundation other than the one already laid, which is Jesus Christ. If any man builds on this foundation using gold, silver, costly stones, wood, hay or straw, his work will be shown for what it is, because the Day will bring it to light. It will be revealed with fire, and the fire will test the quality of each man's work. If what he has built survives, he will receive his reward. If it is burned up, he will suffer loss; he himself will be saved, but only as one escaping through the flames.*

Jesus Christ is our foundation. He is the cornerstone of our faith and spiritual house. Nothing we build is worth anything without Him as our foundation. We can build flimsy walls of straw through laziness, apathy, and neglect; or we can build up walls of gold through obedience, diligence, and good stewardship. Each man's house (symbolic in this verse for his spiritual life) will ultimately be burned, but as we know, straw turns to ash while gold is refined to be even more brilliant. Thank the Lord our salvation is not based on whether our house survives the flames; however, our rewards in heaven are.

Solomon summed it up very poignantly in Ecclesiastes 12:13-14: "Now all has been heard; here is the conclusion of the matter: Fear God and keep his commandments, for this is the whole duty of man. For God will bring every deed into judgment, including every hidden thing, whether it is good or evil." The secret to success in life is simple: obey God. Even the things we do with the door closed will be brought to attention. Can you imagine the world one day knowing all the evil things you did, even in private? This thought should encourage us to live in reverent fear and unswerving integrity.

Now it is time to understand how to apply God's economy to our everyday lives. The application part is difficult but essential in the spiritual growth cycle. In order to transfer theory and head knowledge to real life, we must look for opportunities to challenge us where we are trying to grow. It's like those math problems we had in high school. Doing the problems was tedious, but practicing them over and over prepared us for the test.

We must conform our unique personalities to His systems. We should be clever in how we plan to do this. If we apply a bit of creativity, we can expand our ability to please God in whatever circumstance.

The scriptures given earlier are our guide. The Holy Spirit will now confirm the areas in which we need progress when we let Him probe our hearts. Knowing there is an inevitable accounting gives us a sense of urgency. Businessperson, blue collar worker, educated or not, young or old, men or women, we can all become faithful stewards if we let the Lord begin His work.

The sphere where we carry the most influence is parenthood. Children are little tape recorders running around, remembering everything we say. More than what we say, they notice what we *do*. They are watching how we manage our, household, money, and the time spent with them. They also observe our relationships with others. They can tell right away if something is inconvenient or frustrating to us. If they do not understand why we are doing a particular thing; if possible, we should explain it to them.

If our children see us visiting the sick, writing letters to prisoners, and sharing the gospel, they will quickly learn that life should be spent obeying the Lord's commands and serving others. They can learn compassion, time management, and prioritizing just by watching us.

God gave us our children, so we must value them. They are precious in the Lord's sight. They should never be perceived as headaches or inconveniences (though they might cause them). The best time to begin instilling these lessons is in the early years, but if we have older kids we can always pull them aside and explain things in a loving way. If we appeal to them as an equal, being as humbly transparent as possible, they will be more apt to listen. Honesty builds closeness, and closeness leads to love and reconciliation.

Children learn by example. How can we expect them to tithe or use their money wisely when we do not demonstrate it for them? And it's worse if we tell them one thing and do another. They quickly learn that they cannot trust your word and that those words are pointless. The only example we end up leaving them is hypocrisy. Do you want to raise a bunch of little hypocrites? If not, take care that you back your words with the appropriate action.

Many of us as children worked a lemonade stand, mowed neighbors' lawns, had a newspaper route, or did other work to earn extra cash. We did not realize it then, but those odd jobs taught us important stewardship lessons. We learned the value of the dollar, the discipline to save, and what it means to be a hard worker. If they have not already, encourage your kids to do the same thing. This hands-on business will teach them a lot more than we can by just talking to them.

We have all heard the story of little Johnny touching a hot stove and burning his finger. The pain he felt served to remind him never to touch the hot stove again. So it is in our grownup lives: Making mistakes is a crucial step in the learning process. Mistakes teach us to look at something from a different perspective or to approach a problem from another angle. They keep us humble. Telling our kids about our past mistakes or even admitting the ones we make in front of them will help remind them that their parents are also humans, trying their best to please God. Approaching them as a fellow learner instead of an annoying lecturer will help them respect us more and they will be more apt to listen.

If we want our children to be the next generation that stands for Christ, they must be trained to do so. We all live *in* the world, but we do not have to be *of* the world. Help your children use their talents and abilities for the Lord when they are young. Giving thank you gifts, stuffing bulletins, and even setting up chairs gets children involved in the serving aspect of fellowship. They have a lot of energy at that age anyway, and this will set the stage for learning more stewardship lessons in the future. We want to raise men and women who understand their responsibilities as a child of God and have already had some experience in learning how to carry them out. "Train a child in the way he should go, and when he is old he will not turn from it" (Proverbs 22:6).

As we delve further into the final accounting, we need to remember that God does not hold us accountable for things outside our control. If there is an "unexpected outcome" in the management of our affairs, it may not be an act of poor stewardship.

Suppose we are managing a group of employees or watching over a wealthy man's estate and a severe weather problem or health hazard strikes. These are clearly out of the steward's control. He is not responsible for the demise of the things he is watching over in this case. Now, if there were some warning of a severe storm or horrible epidemic, the steward would have to prepare to a certain degree in hopes of avoiding the potential tragedies. We were reminded of this earlier in Proverbs 22:3. Because the Lord is a fair and righteous judge, we can trust that the accounting will be fair and appropriate. There is no need to walk around with a heavy burden. Sometimes bad things happen and we just have to trust the Lord to help us do our best with what is left over.

Jesus said in Luke 16:10-12 that to whom has been given much, much will be demanded. Have you been given much by God? How much? In what ways? What do you think God expects from you in this life? We need to reflect on these questions in our everyday lives. They help bring overwhelming issues or circumstances back into perspective. Remember, it doesn't have to be something spectacular to hold importance to God. The smallest service matters to the Lord and benefits His economy.

Prayer of Change

Almighty God, help me from now on to become the kind of steward you want me to be. Give me strength by your Spirit to overcome the temptations my flesh may face when I try to be a humble servant. Lord, in everything I do, help me to remember that I am just a manager of your resources and not my own. As I grow in my walk, enable me to accomplish all the tasks you have given me, even if they seem petty. Jesus, thank you for the opportunity to give back to you. In Jesus' name I pray. Amen.

Part 4

CONTENTMENT

LEARNING TO BE CONTENT

Economic Principle:
accepting God's plan without complaint
whatever the circumstances.

I am not saying this because I am in need, for I have learned to be content whatever the circumstances. I know what it is to be in need and I know what it is to have plenty. I have learned the secret of being content in any and every situation, whether well fed or hungry, whether living in plenty or in want. I can do all things through him who gives me strength. Philippians 4:11-13

But godliness with contentment is great gain. For we brought nothing into the world and can take nothing out of it. But if we have food and clothing, we will be content with that. People who want to get rich fall into temptation and a trap and into many foolish and harmful desires that plunge men into ruin and destruction. For the love of money is the root of all kinds of evil. Some people, eager for money, have wandered from the faith and pierced themselves with many griefs. 1 Timothy 6:6-10

Some soldiers were questioning Him, saying, "And what about us, what shall we do?" And he said to them, "Do not take money from anyone by force, or accuse anyone falsely, and be content with your wages." Luke 3:14

For He has satisfied the thirsty soul, and the hungry soul He has filled with what is good. Psalm 107:9

*The fear of the LORD leads to life, so that one may sleep
satisfied, untouched by evil.* Proverbs 19:23

The economic principles God wants us to learn in this section of contentment are diverse. In His economy, the section of contentment is the fourth and final anchor. In the other three anchors we discussed (ownership, giving, and stewardship), we learned critical steps to walking more uprightly on the path towards pleasing God. Focusing now on contentment, we will learn how to round out these lessons in the inner struggles we face every day. Contentment is an attitude that comes from within. If we try our best to do all the other things God has laid out for us without being happy doing them, learning the other lessons are futile.

To really please the Lord we must focus on all four areas, not just one. Living a life of contentment will better help us handle the temptations that inevitably come our way. We can be happy in the circumstance we are in, without letting the devil plant seeds of bitterness and distrust in our hearts. The stronger our foundation, the more we will be prepared for spiritual warfare.

Webster defines contentment as "satisfied, to wait quietly, patience, to appease the desires of; to limit oneself in desires, actions, and requirements. Freedom from care or discomfort. Manifesting satisfaction with one's possessions, status, or situation."

These definitions are great supporters in our understanding, but to get the whole picture, let's look at what contentment is *not*. The dictionary defines *dis*contentment as: "unsatisfied, a malcontent. A restless aspiration for improvement. A sense of grievance. One who is discontented." And what is a malcontent? "One who bears a grudge from a sense of grievance or thwarted ambition. Someone who is dissatisfied with the existing state of affairs."

Now that we know the definitions, it should be easy to apply this to our lives, right? That is hardly the case! There are more financial sins and mistakes because of lack of understanding in this category than in any other part of the economy of God. This is because most people, Christians included, have never learned to be happy with where they are at. In this section we are not learning to just be content in our financial lives, though this is extremely important, but in all areas of life. Single people can be discontented because they long to be married. Married people can long to be single. People strive for higher job titles and raises. Lack of contentment for a Christian can be found in the church if the person is not happy serving where he is placed.

The truth is, it is a lot harder for a person to say, "I'm okay right here, right now." It is more common to hear, "If only this or that would happen in my life, then everything would be fine." This philosophy is a restless evil because it begins to consume the life of the one who harbors it. This is precisely why Proverbs 30:8-9 says to "keep falsehood and lies far from me; give me neither poverty nor riches, but give me only my daily bread. Otherwise, I may have too much and disown you and say, 'Who is the LORD?' Or I may become poor and steal, and so dishonor the name of my God."

Take the cosmetic industry for instance. This is a multibillion dollar industry cashing in on people's contentment problems. Sure you may have a big nose or loose skin, but are you fixing those things just for the sake of image?

Discontentment also causes people to spend and fall into debt and that, of course, ruins relationships. The ambition could be anything: a new car, new clothes, remodeling the house; but is the reason behind it worthy in the Lord's sight? Everyone knows in his heart what will make him feel happier, but what would happen if we did what God says and quit aspiring for more where it is not needed? It is right and biblically correct to have financial goals and objectives, but if we do not reach these goals, can we still be content? Of course we can because the Bible says we can "do all things through Christ who strengthens [us]" (Philippians 4:13). The key point is that we as believers must learn to be content in the present, even if an event we have long been hoping for never happens. It is fine to plan for a college education, owning a home and for retirement. In fact, it is wise, but if this becomes our main focus and life suddenly turns into a keep-up-with-the-Joneses pursuit, we have missed the mark and are living in sin.

You may feel that you've blown it in life because of too many mistakes in this area of contentment due to poor decisions and choices. You may say, "It's hard for me to be content in almost anything because I can be compulsive and impulsive, which gets me into trouble." Be honest before God and tell Him that you want to make some changes in your life. You can receive His forgiveness, grace, and mercy. We are not perfect people; that is why we need to confess our sins and repent to lift the load of guilt. God's never-ending love for us is incredible! When we understand and know what contentment is in the eyes of God, we can find fulfillment in our life on this earth.

I can see why God has us run another lap around the track until we get it right, can't you? The "lap of life," so to speak, is like another circumstance or trial we can learn from. God wants us to listen to Him and be humble in learning true contentment. It is an important biblical lesson that leads us to finding true fulfillment and peace in our hearts. Only a personal relationship with Jesus Christ can fill our hearts with peace which greatly overshadows the "must haves" and "demands" of living on earth.

There is nothing like going through a trial to remind us what it means to be content. As we go through the journeys of life, there are many trials such as losing a job, losing a loved one through divorce or illness, and so on. What is important is how we handle each difficulty we face and our attitude to trust God through it.

A friend, who was going through a hard time with being single and unemployed, said to me, "Tom, it's easy to be content when things are going right and you have a job, a family, and your health, but when those are taken away, I don't think you can feel content as easily." I told him that he's right and that there had also been difficult times in my life when I was angry with God. This is when we need to turn our focus to our heavenly Father and know that He is allowing those trials in our lives to refine us and lead us to true contentment. My friend learned this tool in his life in order to allow God's leading to manage "living life."

Let's take a look at the different economic principles that make up this crucial tool called contentment by seeing what Paul learned from his lessons. In Philippians 4:11-13, he specifically said he had learned the secret of contentment, no matter the situation. This is not something that happened overnight or even when he became a Christian. Rather, it was a process of dealing with difficult circumstances that brought him to the realization that his hope was set on his eternal life with Christ, not his earthly circumstances. Paul is telling us that even in plenty he still had to learn the secret of contentment.

You might ask, "What is there to learn about contentment when you are well off?" Have you ever had a time in your life when you were "living the good life," and you forgot about

God because you thought you had all you needed? Paul's focus was not on the "plenty" but on ministering for the Lord. His value system was on preaching the gospel of Jesus Christ. He knew God would provide for his needs as he defined them in I Timothy 6:6. Some would say it is harder to be content in want rather than in plenty. It could be either, of course, depending on an individual's weakness. Paul explains that he learned contentment in both through Christ. Philippians 4:13 says, "I can do all things through him who gives me strength." Paul trusted God and His sovereign plan, not in his own abilities or strengths. And God was more interested in Paul's character than his comfort.

In Paul's letter to Timothy we see again that "great gain" is defined as godliness with contentment. "For we brought nothing into the world, and we can take nothing out of it" (1 Timothy 6:7). Interesting how Paul says that we came empty-handed and will leave empty-handed. No moving trucks! "But Paul, you mean I'm supposed to be content with just food and clothing?" Second Peter 1:3 tells us that we have been given "everything we need for life and godliness through our knowledge of [Christ]." Paul is communicating to us that godliness is the pursuit of true Christian values and attributes such as the fruit of the spirit (Galatians 5:22). It's about finding satisfaction and peace in God's great promises and learning to accept His will for our lives through all circumstances.

We will have a clearer understanding of God's economy as we move closer toward the virtues of Christ and farther from pursuing riches and earthly desires. "Live by the Spirit, and you will not gratify the desires of the sinful nature," Paul says in Galatians 5:16. The sinful nature's desires and the Spirit's desires are in conflict with each other. Thus, when you feel yourself experiencing a fight between the "angel" and "devil" on your shoulders, remember that if the advice you are inclined to believe is contrary to God's Word, it is not His voice you are hearing.

Prayer of Change

Heavenly Father, I know that more often than not I have an attitude of impatience and bitterness rather than one of contentment. I am sorry that I have impeded your progress in my life because of these attitudes. Lord Jesus, help me to accept the changes in my life that you advocate. I want to be flexible with your plan because your Word promises that it is the most beneficial for me. Jesus, help me to listen to that still small voice rather than my own thoughts and help me to discern which are which. I love you, Jesus, and ask that you help me better glorify you as I learn and apply these lessons. In Jesus' name. Amen.

THE LOVE OF MONEY

Economic Principle:
pursuing money over God.

He who loves money will not be satisfied with money, nor he who loves abundance with its income. This too is vanity. Ecclesiastes 5:10

Do not lay up for yourselves treasures on earth, where moth and rust destroy, and where thieves break in and steal. But lay up for yourselves treasures in heaven, where moth and rust do not destroy, and where thieves do not break in and steal. For where your treasure is, there your heart will be also. Matthew 6:19-21

What will it profit a man if he gains the whole world and forfeits his soul? Or what will a man give in exchange for his soul? Matthew 16:26

People who want to get rich fall into temptation and a trap and into many foolish and harmful desires that plunge men into ruin and destruction. For the love of money is a root of all kinds of evil. Some people, eager for money, have wandered from the faith and pierced themselves with many griefs. 1 Timothy 6:9-10

Behold, the man who would not make God his refuge, but trusted in the abundance of his riches and was strong in his evil desire. Psalm 52:7

Why are so many rich people discontent with life? After all, don't they have "everything" one could want? Can a rich Christian be discontent, too, or is this term for non-believers only?

Paul is warning us that the opposite side of godliness with contentment is the love of money and the desire to be rich. First Timothy 6:10 does not say that *money* is evil, but that the *love* of it is. This love of money is the catalyst to many downfalls. It is the "root of all sorts of evil." It causes "some people, eager for money [to wander] from the faith and [pierce] themselves with many griefs." This passage also says that people who want to get rich plunge themselves into ruin and destruction. Can it get any more graphic? Matthew 6:19-20 says, "Do not lay up for yourselves treasures on earth, where moth and rust destroy, and where thieves break in and steal. But lay up for yourselves treasures in heaven."

If you are thinking, "Tom, it's too late, I've already wandered," remember that it is never too late if you want to come back to God! If you have truly repented and your motives are changed, the Lord will surely welcome you back to the fold because He loves you. The prodigal son never deserved the special treatment he received after being so ungrateful, but his father forgave him and welcomed him home. God wants us to come home and pursue contentment rather than finding discontentment in the love of money, covetousness, worldly wealth, and materialism. Hebrews 13:5 tell us, "Make sure that your character is free from the love of money, being content with what you have; for He Himself has said: 'I will never desert you, nor will I ever forsake you." This is just another reminder to be content with what we have. God will never leave our side. What a blessing to know how much He cares for us!

The economic principle of contentment in Proverbs 16:8 also instructs us to be pleased or content with a small amount of income or assets earned righteously more than a large income resulting from sin or injustice. This teaching is designed to draw boundaries for us to live within. In the economy of God we must have limits to help establish rules and controls to conduct our life. Otherwise, we would end up like the world, pursuing as much wealth as we deemed necessary. With no limitations, we would lead ourselves down the road of self-gratification which always leads to hell.

In addition, doing things God's way is less painful and gives us less to worry about. If we exercise integrity in everything we do, we never have to worry about someone accusing us of wrongdoing. Cheaters live their lives constantly looking behind them, hoping no one catches them. The honest person is more content because he does not have to look over his shoulder at all!

By obeying God, we can be fulfilled in our financial life even if our personal financial goals are never achieved. A goal is great to have for financial planning purposes, but it is not the "end all" so that if it is not attained our world comes crashing down on us. Things like depression and anxiety that accompany unattained financial goals are like the warning lights on our car's dashboard that alert us something is wrong under the hood. Our hope is not based on things of this world. Unbelievers put all their eggs into one basket, never realizing there are gaping holes on the bottom. Christ holds all believer's eggs in His basket—a basket with an unyielding foundation of promises.

Obedience to God brings us fulfillment and satisfaction. He wants to satisfy us with Himself. He wants us to come to the point where we desire the things He desires and are content in Him. He is enough to meet the deepest longings of our hearts. The Lord even promises a good night's sleep to those who fear Him and seek to please Him (Proverbs 19:23).

Being content in God's economy means that we can better love others because we know that our deepest needs—both physically and spiritually—are already met. No need for manipulation. We have what we need from the Lord. Our focus can now be on ministry and loving others. Sure, it's a lifelong process as we walk with Christ in obedience, but true contentment means that we don't need to have certain things happen in our lives to be satisfied. So, if someone asks you, "What would it take for you to be really happy?" tell them (only if you really think this) that the answer is "nothing." Then explain why and it will minister to them.

None of us are the wealthiest in terms of worldly values, but we need what God knows we need. That's good enough for me in the economy of God! Proverbs 30:8 exclaims, "Give me neither poverty nor riches!" It's not easy when God says no to our requests, but His ways are not our ways and He knows best. Although He always answers the prayers of those who come to Him with a humble heart, He never promises to answer them the way we might expect or desire. We must be content with His decisions, even though we do not receive what we were hoping for. Those hopes must never turn into demands towards God. It is critical to watch our anger and check our attitudes. Our dreams must be put in front of God at the altar, trusting Him for His plan for each of us. Remember he loves you with all of His heart, forever and ever.

Prayer of Change

Dear Jesus, I understand that you can satisfy my longings better than any worldly thing can. You give me water that quenches my thirst forever. I want to long after this kind of fulfillment, so please feed my desire for spiritual enrichment. I trust you, Father. In Jesus' name. Amen.

GREED

Economic Principle:
being greedy.

Riches do not profit in the day of wrath, but righteousness delivers from death. Proverbs 11:4

Let him not trust in emptiness, deceiving himself; for emptiness will be his reward. Job 15:31

Do not be afraid when a man becomes rich, when the glory of his house is increased: For when he dies he will carry nothing away; his glory will not descend after him. Psalm 49:16-17

He who trusts in his riches will fall, but the righteous will flourish like the green leaf. Proverbs 11:28

A rich man's wealth is his strong city, and like a high wall in his own imagination. Proverbs 18:11

I have seen all the works which have been done under the sun, and behold, all is vanity and striving after wind. Ecclesiastes 1:14

I said to myself, "Come now, I will test you with pleasure. So enjoy yourself." And behold, it too was futility. Ecclesiastes 2:1

I completely despaired of all the fruit of my labor for which I had labored under the sun. Ecclesiastes 2:20

I collected for myself silver and gold and the treasure of kings and provinces. I provided for myself male and female singers and the pleasures of men—many concubines. Then I became great and increased more than all who preceded me in Jerusalem. My wisdom also stood by me. All that my eyes desired I did not refuse them. I did not withhold my heart from any pleasure, for my heart was pleased because of all my labor and this was my reward for all my labor. Thus I considered all my activities which my hands had done and the labor which I had exerted, and behold all was vanity and striving after wind and there was no profit under the sun. Ecclesiastes 2:8-11

As he had come naked from his mother's womb, so he will return as he came. He will take nothing from the fruit of his labor that he can carry in his hand. Ecclesiastes 5:15

All a man's labor is for his mouth and yet the appetite is not satisfied. Ecclesiastes 6:7

Men prepare a meal for enjoyment, and wine makes life merry, and money is the answer to everything. Ecclesiastes 10:19

Jesus said to His disciples, "Truly I say to you, it is hard for a rich man to enter the kingdom of heaven." Matthew 19:23

Woe to you who are rich, for you are receiving your comfort in full. Luke 6:24

The righteousness of the upright will deliver them, but the treacherous will be caught by their own greed. Proverbs 11:6

He said to them, "Beware, and be on your guard against every form of greed; for not even when one has an abundance does his life consist of his possessions." And He told them a parable, saying, "The land of a certain rich man was very productive. And he began reasoning to himself, saying, 'What shall I do, since I have no place to store my crops?' Then he said, 'This is what I will do: I will tear down my barns and build larger ones, and there I will store all my grain and all my goods. And I will say to my soul, "Soul, you have many goods laid up for many years to come; take your ease, eat, drink, and be merry.' " But God said to him, "You fool! This very night your soul is required of you; and now who will own what you have prepared?" So is the man who lays up treasure for himself and is not rich toward God. Luke 12:15-21

What is the source of quarrels and conflicts among you? Is not the source your pleasures that wage war in your members? You lust and do not have; so you commit murder. And you are envious and cannot obtain; so you fight and quarrel. You do not have because you do not ask. You ask and do not receive, because you ask with the wrong motives, so that you may spend it on your pleasures.
James 4:1-3

There are many economic principles in the economy of God that pertain to the scriptures above. In going through the Bible book by book, we find many interesting lessons from God. By cross-referencing these verses with other verses from both the Old and New Testaments, we can make no mistake on God's intent. If He says it, it stands.

What is so great about the Bible is that we do not have to go to seminary or graduate school to understand it. God did not bring salvation only to the educated. He wants everyone to understand the lesson He is teaching. So let's start by going through the dictionary and reiterating the meanings of words we do not understand, like greed, wantonness, and acquisitiveness. Then there can be no misunderstanding as to why they are sins.

Webster's definitions:

1. acquisitiveness: strongly desirous of acquiring and possessing
2. greed: excessive or reprehensible acquisitiveness
3. avarice: excessive or insatiable desire for wealth or gain

Lavishness is not God's norm, nor is poverty. But affluence does present a threat for Christians in their walk with the Lord—primarily because they begin to trust in their wealth as though it were their own and as though it were their source of security and worth. Remember from the previous section on ownership that this attitude steals away God's authority and supremacy in our lives. However, not *all* Christians tend to this attitude. There are many wealthy believers who use their assets for God's work and support ministries through their generosity.

So for those of us who can stand to be reminded—and that includes everyone—the lessons are clear: Do not be greedy, do not love money, do not trust in your wealth, do not pursue riches at the sacrifice of relationships, and do not become conceited because of many assets.

Solomon expounded on the futility of riches in the book Ecclesiastes. He had more than everything he could have ever wanted, but he was not happy. He knew no amount of money could ever buy contentment, satisfaction, or peace of mind. Those things come from wisdom, forgiveness, obedience, and love—the things God values.

Another interesting point springs from the verses in Timothy: Anyone eager for money plunges himself into ruin by choosing to idolize money over God. They willingly subject themselves to the darkness when the light is shining right in front of them. The love of money is the root of all kinds of evil because it pushes aside the deity of the Lord and heightens man's selfish desires. *Money* is not the problem, it is the heart behind the lips that kiss it that God abhors. That is why Jesus said it would be so hard for a rich man to enter heaven. Not that he is incapable of entering, just that it is *very* difficult.

In addition to the love of money, get-rich-quick schemes have tainted America's view of not only providential trust, but also hard work. People fall prey to infomercials promising them fast money in return for being lazy. They would rather sit in misery watching those pathetic shows than to get up and work, trusting God to provide. Everyone loves quick money, we hardly have to work for it, but the "quick fix" to the financial problem will not repair the underlying emotional problem. Our value system and personal worth are not related at all to our wealth. Having money does not mean that you are a successful person in God's economy. A person's worth must be based on who they *are* in Christ, because apart from Him they are nothing. No wonder we *feel* like nothing without Him!

In order to live God's way, we must examine Scripture and change our lifestyle accordingly. There is no doubt that this can be difficult, especially living in a society where the American Dream is so prevalent.

What exactly is the American Dream? Every person has his own definition. Some see it as having a large house, pool, and RV. Others say it is having a CEO position and making lots of money. Still others believe it is all about a good retirement package where work is minimal. With so many different views on a successful life, we must let God's Word be our central compass. All it takes is for one thing to go wrong and we know that our own plans do not always succeed. But God's plan does—if we let it. His dream for us is far better than anything we could have conjured up, and that dream can become reality if we stick to living within our means and letting Him direct us.

One practical way we can monitor our heart and its motivations is to keep a spending journal. Writing down our expenditures shows us where our "drive" for a certain thing comes from. After a month, we can see that we spent over $500 on clothes, or that we are continually buying new equipment for our stereo system. These seem like trivial examples, but keeping a journal opens our eyes to the fact that we have a problem with greed. Everyone who claims Jesus Christ is his Lord and Savior has an obligation to listen to God's economy and change the way he lives.

Remember, money in itself is not evil. It is simply a mode of exchange, a currency. The sinful aspect comes when we use money as a way of carrying out our evil desires, albeit envy, greed, jealousy, selfish ambition, or any other instance where we can see it working in our advantage.

Do you want to be a beautiful person in God's sight? When He looks upon your heart, do you want it to be pure and blameless? Do you want the peace that passes understanding to inundate your entire existence? Then love the Lord your God with all your heart, your soul, your mind, and your strength. This is beautiful in His economy.

Prayer of Change

Lord, search my heart for any thoughts or desires that do not honor you. Bring them to my attention so that I can confess and repent. Help me to clearly see what I say and do and how it affects others, my life, and your glory in the future. Help me to be open and honest with the Holy Spirit, choosing to be obedient to His promptings. Lord, instill in my heart the proper goals that will help me carry out your will for my life. I understand that my plans may be good, but yours are far better. I hereby submit to you as the clay, willing to be molded by the Potter and used for your glory in any way you deem appropriate. Take away my sources of greed and materialism that prevent me from giving my all to you. In Jesus' name I pray. Amen.

A LESSON FROM PAUL

Economic Principle:
learn through Paul's application.

I am not saying this because I am in need, for I have learned to be content whatever the circumstances. I know what it is to be in need, and I know what it is to have plenty. I have learned the secret of being content in any and every situation, whether well fed or hungry, whether living in plenty or in want. I can do all things through him who gives me strength. Philippians 4:11-13

When learning how to understand and apply the principles of contentment inside the economy of God, we must begin with our great Teacher, and then we need to pray. Prayer is essential if one wants to be content because through it we put our total dependence on the Lord. He is faithful to answer us, and He promises to teach us through the good and bad experiences of life. Philippians 4:6 says, "Be anxious for nothing, but in everything by prayer and supplication with thanksgiving let your requests be made known to God."

Look at the apostle Paul's life. He spent hours in prayer over the unnerving circumstances in his life. Spending time in prayer gave him a godly perspective. He compared each situation to his walk with God. Because Paul's personal worth came from knowing, being grounded in, and growing in Jesus Christ, nothing could destroy him. He knew that God's will for his life was ultimately determined by God's plan for him: how long he lived, where he lived, under what conditions, and his purpose.

This is why God is our Teacher. He specifically uses His plan for us to teach us important truths. Blowing a job interview, losing a mate, having less than what we think necessary to live on, becoming ill, and being rejected by loved ones all bring us back to reality; but that reality is that through whatever situation we are in, God wants us to learn something new about His character. These situations bring light to our weaknesses, but that is where the Lord's strength is best exhibited. "When I am weak, then am I strong" (2 Corinthians 12:10).

Paul learned to be content whatever the circumstance because his focus and attitude was on living for Christ. His dependence was on the Holy Spirit for direction (Galatians 6:8), rather than his job success or gaining wealth. We will not learn contentment if we do not place God first in our life.

I asked a friend one day, "Do you identify your life with being a successful dentist?" He said that he did and that he would not know what he would do if he lost the dental practice or his ability to be a dentist. My friend's profession is his image to society and what people know him to be. If that is stripped away, would all be lost? To some people, yes, because that is all they depend on in life. In God's economy, He wants us to grow in His image, not the world's. He wants to strip away the things of the flesh and give us the things of the Spirit.

The fruit of the spirit is love, joy, peace, patience, and so on. We are not in control of life's circumstances and we cannot hold on so tightly that we set ourselves up for a major fall should there be disappointment or financial disaster. God is more concerned about who we are than what we do. Our reputation and success must be first in our relationship with Jesus Christ. By knowing we cannot lose that because our eternity is secure, we can go through hardships that change us for our ultimate good.

Yet, we cannot deny that there is pain and suffering on this earth. Every day we hear in the news of the terrible circumstances that happen to people. There is no doubt that until we get to heaven, bad things will continue to happen in this life. When we go through a financial or health crisis, we need to focus on the purpose God has for our life. Are we going to live for possessions and popularity? Are we going to be driven by the pressures of life? Guilt? Bitterness? Materialism? There is always something good we can thank God for. Let's focus on our purpose rather than our problems and keep our eyes on the right goals.

When reading the following list, think about whether any of the incidences mentioned would make you feel happier. What would it take to be "really happy"? Be honest with yourself and check which ones apply.

I would be truly happy in life if:

1. I could get married
2. I could get divorced
3. I could be rich
4. My child was healed from illness
5. I was healed from illness
6. I could get a particular job
7. I could get out of debt
8. I could retire financially independent
9. I could get revenge
10. I could become famous

You see, if it takes any of these things to happen for you to be content, then you are truly not content. That does not mean that having goals and plans prove us to be discontent, but it does mean that if those desires are never met, we are happy in knowing that Jesus Christ is enough for us and that God has a better plan for us than we do ourselves.

Let's look at another list, and this time, ask yourself which of these incidences could happen and your contentment in Christ would remain the same.

I will be content in my relationship with Christ even if:

1. I am diagnosed with a terminal illness
2. My spouse or child becomes ill
3. My spouse or child suddenly dies
4. I get laid off
5. My spouse leaves and files for divorce
6. My boyfriend/girlfriend breaks up with me
7. My investment portfolio crashes
8. My company relocates me to a lonely location
9. My children disown me
10. My friends cut all ties
11. I can't get a raise/job
12. I never get married
13. My friends/enemies slander me
14. I lose my home

Many of us have experienced these kinds of tragedies and unfair circumstances as well. My wife and I have seen people who have wrongfully been imprisoned but they are still able to serve Christ behind bars. Some people who go through a divorce suffer unfair custody issues. Does God still care? Yes, and He does have a plan for our lives. We must remember that God is our provider and will meet our needs. Let's become the type of Christians that are great stewards and generous givers, serving Christ every day and ministering to others (Galatians 6:8-9). We can enjoy life while still learning what it means to be content and satisfied. Everyone would like to have more "stuff" in life, but if we have the tools to learn the most difficult spiritual lessons of living, we can be content. Do we really want that in our life and to grow in Him? Let the Holy Spirit search our hearts for that answer now and take a minute to respond to God in prayer.

Prayer of Change

Father God, teach me what it means to be content. Lord, help me not to covet money, fame, or anything else that would cause you to become second or third in my life. I want to take the time right now to confess and repent of my sin of discontentment. I recognize that you have blessed me, and I want to be truly happy where I am. So search my heart, Lord, and help me rid my soul of all the aimless pursuits I try so desperately to hold onto. Teach me how to keep my financial and life goals intact without letting them rule my life. Give me wisdom to know and discern contentment. Thank you for your love and mercy. Lord, help me to minister to others to be content in you alone. I praise you for blessing me with joy and peace! I praise you, Jesus, for blessing me with so much! You truly are a God of wonders! Continue to work a miracle in me! In Jesus' name I pray. Amen.

Part 5

CONCLUSION

OVERVIEW OF THE FOUR ANCHORS

If we were to sum up this book in a nutshell, we would say that to know the economy of God is to understand that the Lord is the supreme owner of everything, and life is simply about learning to give back to God while having a good attitude. If any of these areas suffers—ownership, giving, stewardship, and contentment—then they all suffer. Understanding how these principles intermingle is like comparing it to a well-oiled machine. When all the parts are carefully maintained, the machine can reach its highest output level. Living in the economy of God is no exception: If we have a sour attitude while working, we drag ourselves down. Not only are we miserable, but we miss the opportunity to reach our potential. When these four areas are consistently monitored and improved, however, we bring glory to God and we experience a deep, satisfying joy. There is no possible way we can reach perfection in this life because we are still living in the sin nature. But when we meet Jesus, our understanding and character will be perfectly complete.

So what's the point of striving to be more Christ-like if we will eventually be perfect? Well, the first reason is because God said to. Obedience is the number one God-pleaser in His economy. He is more delighted with obedience than with sacrifice (1 Samuel 15:22). The second reason for striving for Christ-likeness is because it earns us rewards in heaven. The rewards are not specifically described in Scripture, but they are said to include crowns and inexplicable joy. Though obedience alone is reason enough to refine our character, knowing there are future rewards provides a special incentive to motivate us to action.

So as you begin this daily journey, let me leave you with a few words of encouragement. If you read this book and realize you have lots of work ahead of you, don't be discouraged! Find the areas that need the most improvement and commit to starting there. These issues take lifetimes to work out so don't expect a miracle overnight. Baby steps are the key. If you are convicted about the lack of prayer in your life, start tackling that problem by opening the lines of communication. This way the Lord will be able to reveal more areas down the road.

Sit down and make a list of all the areas you need to work on, and then prioritize them. If this is confusing or overwhelming in any way, remember I am available for help and so are those at Crown Ministries.

Most of all, remember that the Lord is your number one fan! He wants to see you succeed more than any other person on the planet. He wants to see you at your godliest. Give Him the opportunity to challenge and refine you and you will never regret it.

A HEAVENLY INVITATION

If in the reading of this book, you have realized that Christ is not the Lord of your life, it is not too late to accept Him.

First you must understand that without the blood of Christ, you are a sinner in His eyes. The Bible says that "all have sinned and fall short of the glory of God" (Romans 3:23). There is absolutely no way we could ever obtain heaven through good works (Ephesians 2:8-9); rather, it is God who chooses us (Titus 3:5). When we were the most depraved humans possible, in the epitome of our wickedness, this is when Jesus chose to die (Romans 5:8). He loves us with a love we cannot comprehend; however, He is righteous and will not let just anybody into heaven. According to God's holy law, He demands a blood sacrifice to atone for sin (Hebrews 9:22), but even if we were to shed our own blood it would only be filth in His eyes because our blood is tainted with sin. Because God is perfect and holy in 100 percent of His being, He demands something just as perfect to redeem a broken covenant.

It was the Master's plan since the creation of the world to provide us with a way to spend eternity with Him—and that plan includes His Son Jesus Christ. There is no other way a man can be saved (John 14:6). His blood on the cross was holy enough to appease God's demand for a blood sacrifice (1 Peter 1:19) because he was 100 percent man and 100 percent God.

Now we have a way to heaven, but we must accept it and believe that Christ's blood was perfect enough to pay our debt on the cross, or we will live in hell. God will not make us repent; we must choose to do it on our own. But if we do repent (repenting means to make a 180-degree turn and forsake our evil ways), we are promised a clean spirit (Acts 3:19).

Repenting also involves confession. Romans 10:9-10 says that we believe in our heart, but confession must be made with the mouth. In other words, simply believing Jesus is God and that He died on the cross is not enough. There must be a verbal acknowledging. The Lord knows a pure heart, so if true confession is made, forgiveness is automatic (1 John 1:9).

If this all makes sense and you would like to take these steps, you can do so now. Talk to God. The first prayer He hears is the sinner's prayer. Explain to Him that you understand salvation is a free, undeserved gift. Tell him you accept Jesus' sacrifice as your own and now you want to glorify Him.

Once you have done these things, know that there are promises for believers. God gave us His Son for salvation and He will never take Him away (1 John 5:11-13). No matter how many times you sin, if you have truly repented, you have eternal life (John 5:24).

The Lord also gives His children a portion of His Spirit as a deposit guaranteeing the good things to come (Ephesians 1:14). His Spirit is an ever-present guide and acts as our conscience to help us live a life pleasing to God. If we feel the prick of the Holy Spirit when we sin or are thinking of sinning, we know He lives in us (1 John 3:24). This is another way to be assured of our salvation.

Lastly, you must know that we are saved for a purpose. God certainly delights in our redemption, but He is more pleased when we bring Him glory. We have been saved through Him, for Him, and to honor Him (Ephesians 2:10; Colossians 1:16). This book covers many of the specifics on how to please the Lord, but above all, God delights in obedience. So the more we know what He asks us to do and who He wants us to become, the better we can obey (1 Samuel 15:22). Fellow brother and sister, study the Scriptures and the Lord will bless you with every spiritual blessing and guide you on the path to righteousness.

The Heavenly Invitation

Dear reader,

You are cordially invited to receive Jesus Christ as your Lord and Savior on this very day _____. Please RSVP by saying this prayer for Salvation in your heart:

Lord Jesus, I know that I am a lost sinner. I realize that I do not deserve heaven, but in your great mercy you provided me a way to return to you when you died on the cross and rose again. I believe that your sacrifice was enough to pay the price that I owe and for all mankind. I receive you, Jesus Christ, into my heart and soul. Come into my life and take control. I now repent of my sins and place my trust in you for eternal life. I accept your free gift, understanding that I have done nothing to earn it on my own or by any good works. Help me to serve you now and obey the commandments of the Bible.

Thank you for this incredible gift of grace, and thank you for forgiving me of my sins and preparing a place for me in heaven, secured by your promise. I know that I am forever a part of your family.

In Jesus' name. Amen.

THE WARRANTY AND GUARANTEE OF GOD

A written assurance by God in His economy for all believers

If you know Jesus Christ as your Lord and Savior, you are blessed with the following promise from our Almighty God. His own words describe His promise that can never be broken or taken back. You never have to worry about losing your salvation even if you have committed a sin. Read below what God has to say about salvation once and for all!

A guarantee of eternal life in heaven forever

For with the heart a person believes, resulting in righteousness, and with the mouth he confesses, resulting in salvation…For whoever will call on the name of the Lord shall be saved. Romans 10:10,13

These things I have written to you…that you may know that you have eternal life. 1 John 5:13

The gift of God is eternal life in Jesus Christ our Lord. Romans 6:23

For by grace you have been saved through faith; and not of yourselves, it is the gift of God; not as a result of works, so that no one should boast. Ephesians 2:8-9

Believe in the Lord Jesus, and you will be saved. Acts 16:31

I say to you, he who believes [in Me] has eternal life.
John 6:47

*If we confess our sins, he is faithful and just and will
forgive us our sins and purify us from all unrighteous-
ness.* 1 John 1:9

*For God so loved the world that he gave his one and
only Son, that whosoever believes in him shall not perish but have everlasting life.* John 3:16

THE WIDOW'S MITE

Sculpted steps of ivory,
Tall pillars of gold,
God's temple in Jerusalem
Was a sight to behold.
But she didn't belong there,
Among the fortune and the fame;
Not with tattered clothes,
Sunken eyes, and a left leg lame.
Her dress and countenance
Were dirty and poor,
A widow rejected,
Usually begging at a door.
Her days were spent
Washing and cleaning,
Salvaging scraps or a
Neighbor's yard gleaning;
Until the day
Her ears heard the man
Claiming to be
The Great I AM.
She knew she should listen,
He spoke words so true;
He told her things
She thought no one knew.
So she followed His lead
Morning and night,
Learning He was the Christ,
God's one true Light.
Her pockets were empty,

Hunger sharp like a knife,
But He satisfied her needs
With the Bread of Life.
His plan of salvation
Was peaceful and free;
Hope she could afford
Since she had no money.
One day she spotted
One small coin on the ground,
To a beggar it was
A treasured well-found.
Her sunken eyes sparkled,
Joy flooded her face;
She knew her Provider,
The great Giver of Grace.
Suddenly an idea,
Her gratitude she'd show;
Her step became light
And off she did go.
Hurrying to the temple,
For it was almost midday;
No force, save for God,
Could keep her away.
Eyes focused on her goal,
The tithing box in sight,
She climbed the stairs
Clutching her mite.
By the large crowd of people
She was pushed to the side,
But she stepped toward the box
And dropped the coin inside.
Jesus was there

And He saw her small deed;
He smiled warmly,
Certainly well-pleased.
When she turned to go
Unaware of His spy,
She suddenly felt
His watchful eye.
His disciples were there
Standing around
When Jesus spoke
Saying something profound.
Though she saw His lips
Moving with care
She made out no words
Paralyzed by His stare.
Jesus saw her action
And gave an approving nod,
For He knew she understood
The Economy of God.

—Heidi Hancock

Thomas V. Meaglia, ChFC
Chartered Financial Consultant and Business Owner

Tom Meaglia has been working in the financial planning business for 28 years and is a financial seminar speaker to churches, non-profit organizations and business owners. Tom specializes in personal financial counseling from a biblical perspective. His consulting and coaching services help people to determine strategies for living by applying God's principles for handling money.

Tom began his career in the financial services industry after graduating from Cal Poly Pomona in 1979 with a degree in Business Administration. He pursued the securities industry and worked as vice-president for firms such as EF Hutton and Kemper Securities. His credentials include ChFC (Chartered Financial Consultant), CLU (Chartered Life Underwriter), IAR (Investment Advisor Representative), and AEP (Accredited Estate Planner). He also has a master's degree, MSFS, (Masters of Science in Financial Services) from the American College. Tom has been an adjunct professor for the School of Business at both, Azusa Pacific and Biola Universities. He currently serves as a board member for OPARC, a non-profit organization that helps support people with disabilities. His ministry to help people with money management includes volunteering as a certified Crown referral coach for Crown Ministries (www.crown.org).

While developing his own business, Meaglia Financial Planning, he continued studying financial principles from the Bible and teaching seminars. Tom's passion to encourage Christians to be great stewards of their finances led him to the vision to write this book which comes from his own journey of life experiences through counseling, teaching and speaking. In 1987, he started hosting a radio talk show program on KKLA 99.5 FM in Southern California called "Financial Strategies for the 90's. His current program on KKLA, "Knowing the Economy of God," airs on Saturdays at 3:30 p.m. He conducts many financial seminars for individuals, businesses, and churches. Tom lives in La Verne, California with his wife, Julie and two children, Melissa & Jonathan.

For more information on seminars and workshops go to his website, www.theeconomyofgod.com or to speak with Tom, call 1-800-386-3700.

Meaglia Financial Planning

114 N. Glendora Avenue, Suite 229

Glendora, CA 91741

Phone: (909) 593-6105

Toll-free: (800) 386-3700

Cell phone: (818) 681-8600 ® Fax: (909) 593-6120

E-mail: tom@theecomomyofgod.com

Web site address: www.theEconomyofGod.com

Knowing the Economy of God
Conference and Workshops

Did you know that God has created and set up His own economic system for our world?

Do you want to know more about God's economy and how it works?

Would you like to learn how to live it in your daily life and experience the peace and financial freedom that God's economy can give you?

"Knowing the Economy of God," presented by Tom Meaglia, speaker, financial counselor, experienced business professional and author, will help people to apply biblical wisdom to their life and understand the four anchors of God's economy.

You can hear Tom's radio program, "Knowing the Economy of God" on KKLA 99.5FM at 3:30 p.m. every Saturday. Tune in to hear a new topic each week or go to www.theEconomyofGod.com to listen to the program online.

Visit www. theEconomyofGod.com to see the financial stewardship topics that Tom can offer to your church.

Plan now for your upcoming conferences and call 1-800-386-3700 for more information or e-mail: tom@theeconomyofgod.com

Knowing the Economy of God
Order Form

For Online orders visit us at: www.theeconomyofgod.com
(credit cards accepted) or call 1-800-386-3700

E-mail: tom@theeconomyofgod.com

Postal orders: Meaglia Financial Planning
       Tom Meaglia
       114 N. Glendora Avenue, Suite 229
       Glendora, CA 91741-3341

Please send *Knowing the Economy of God* to:

Name: _____

Address: _____

City: _____ State: _____

Zip: _____ Telephone: (_____) _____

Book Price: $15.95

Shipping: $3.00 for the first book and $1.00 for each additional book to cover
shipping and handling within US, Canada, and Mexico. International
orders add $6.00 for the first book and $2.00 for each additional book.

or

you can also order our book on Amazon.com
or contact your local bookstore